ATTRACTING
BACKYARD
WILDLIFE

A GUIDE FOR NATURE-LOVERS

D1451706

Voyageur Press

Edited by Brian Scrivener
Cover illustration by Allester Bradbury
Cover design by Brad Nickason
Interior design by Bob English

Typeset at The Typeworks, Vancouver

Printed and bound in Canada by Friesen Printers, Altona, Manitoba

Library of Congress Cataloging-in Publication Data
Merilees, William J.
  Attracting backyard wildlife.

  Bibliography:
  Includes index.

  1. Wildlife attracting.   2. Gardening to attract
wildlife.   I. Title.
QL59.M47 1989   639.9'2   89-5516
ISBN 0-89658-130-6

Contents

Tables

Plates

Foreword

The ideas suggested in this book had their beginning when I was a very young boy. My father and I built quite a number of bird houses and bird feeders for use in our garden. One of our first bird houses produced a family of House Sparrows which gave great delight. One winter our feeders were visited by twelve different bird species. Accepting the challenge to improve on this total gave me additional pleasure. In my late teens, bird banding was a real interest. To make our garden more attractive many native trees and shrubs were planted. During my university years, a class project provided the information for the illustration on approach routes and feeding locations of common winter birds.

Putting these ideas down on paper started in 1974 during graduate studies in Colorado where Ron Ryder introduced me to non-game management and the then-new program of the National Wildlife Federation, "Invite Wildlife to Your Backyard". By this time, my interest in natural history had broadened to just about every type of animal and all the flowering plants.

When the Federation of British Columbia Naturalists received a grant from the British Columbia Ministry of the Environment, Public Conservation Assistance Fund, I was keen to participate. Although it has taken much longer than anticipated, the ideas contained in this book have largely come from my own experience. Both my backyard and that of my parents have been the testing grounds.

No matter how much is written, there will always be new ideas and perspectives on every aspect of wildlife gardening. Since this book has gone to press a number of good ideas have come to hand. These I will have to work on for the future.

Being able to put some ideas down on paper and sharing these with others is my pleasure.

Bill Merilees
Nanaimo, B.C.
December, 1988

Dedication

To my father and mother, Welborne and Eva Merilees who, from my earliest recollections, initiated and kindled an interest in doing things for backyard wildlife. Many of their ideas grace these pages.

Preface

"The world is so full of a number of things
I'm sure we should all be as happy as kings"

R.L.S.

When Robert Louis Stevenson wrote his poem "Happy Thought" he might well have been describing the naturalist living in North America. This corner of the world, so richly endowed with plant and animal species, offers tremendous challenge to any person interested in nature.

As we strive for a quality life style in the 1990's, green areas in the form of parks, gardens, greenbelts, footpaths, and recreation areas remain important to our sense of well being. However, powerful forces are active in all our communities which steadily encroach on all lands green and vacant. Under the banners of 'urban renewal', 'revitalization', 'progress', and similar euphemisms, open space, green space, and wild space is disappearing. One must question the wisdom of this trend, as artificial and more sterile environments become the norm. While every new development provides some greenery, the value of this dressing, from a wildlife perspective, is usually negligible.

Ensuring that wildlife continues to have a place in all our lives begins with an informed public. While city planners and elected officials have a civic duty and the power to ensure each neighborhood has adequate green space, there is no reason why each of us cannot contribute our small share.

Even within our most urban settings, a small oasis of greenery has the potential to become a home to a surprising diversity of life. This oasis may be as small as a balcony garden, or even a window box. With a little imagination and careful planning the attractiveness of even these smallest areas can be improved, and a surprising array of insects, birds, and other animals will feel welcome. In fact, some species appear to thrive in urban situations. The simple joy each new species brings the observer cannot be measured in dollars and cents.

The measure of enjoyment can only be appreciated as a warm feeling within.

The aim of this book is to provide some simple ideas that will assist us in improving our gardens and living environments for wildlife.

"Wildlife", as I use the term, means all things, living and wild, from crickets to bats. While this scale might appear very broad, it is well to remember that all living creatures have similar needs. Providing for one species invariably benefits others.

As you proceed to develop your wildlife oasis 'Good Luck' and more important, have fun and enjoy doing it. Along the way share your ideas with others. I am ever willing to hear of your successes and suggestions. After all, trial and error leads to perfection.

Acknowledgements

In a formal sense this project began when the Federation of British Columbia Naturalists and the first appointee to the Urban Wildlife Section of the British Columbia Fish and Wildlife Branch, Ministry of the Environment, met to come up with ways of fostering interest in urban wildlife. Through the Ministry's Public Conservation Assistance Fund, money was provided to assist preparation of this manuscript.

I am greatly indebted to the Ministry and to Bert Brink and Jude Grass of the Federation for their interest and assistance in this project.

The following members of the Federation provided information during the formative stages: Jack Sarles, Mildred McPhee, Blair Smith, George Newell, Peter Van Kerkoerle, A. M. Dahlke, Wilma Robinson, Jim and Joan Burbridge, Billie Steele, Cy Morehen, Martha Harding, Mary-Louise Macdonald, Madelon Schouten, Daphne Smith, Eileen Tuomaala, Jack Williams, Rob Cannings, Emerson Reid, Seff Wilson, Wayne Erickson, Maurice Ellison, John and Helen Agg, Trudy Pastrick, A. Wall, Donna Underhill, Jim and Hazel Street, Mary Palmer, Audrey Sugden, June Cuming, Helen Watson, Bernice Ashlee, Katherine Capes, Ian Hamilton, Jane Perrin, Tessa Campbell, Jim Grant, Enid and Jack Gillis, Pat Swift, Nancy Serra, Frank and Mary Paul, Tom and Mary Collins, Malcolm Martin, Wayne Stetski, and Susan Yates.

Special thanks are due to David Stirling, Yorke Edwards, Harold Pollock, and Larry Halverson for materials provided during the writing stages.

Collen Henson, Philip Hopewell, Helen Gregory, and staff at the Royal British Columbia Museum helped compile the bird nesting information.

Illustrative materials were provided by Doug Kragh, Chris Tunnock, Allyson MacBean, Al Grass, and Bertha McHaffie-Gow.

I am especially grateful to the following people for their technical advice and assistance: Liz Thundstrom, Wildlife Rescue Association of British Columbia; Lee Webb, Siskiyou National Forest; Bill Haight, Oregon Department of Fish and Wildlife; Mike Houck, Portland Audubon Society; Stephen Penland, Washington Department of Wildlife; Dr. Ken Langelier, Veterinarian; and Brian Herrin, Teacher and amateur entomologist.

Bruce Whitington, David Stirling, Allan Murray, and Brian Scrivener provided valued editorial assistance.

Typing, word processing, and rough editing were graciously provided by Sandra Lawrence, Jude Grass, and Patricia Robison.

Last, but far from least, is my appreciation to June who, through all stages, has been my sounding board and spell-checker.

To all the above, my thanks.

1

Introducing Wildlife Gardening: Needs and Considerations

A recent report for the Canadian Wildlife Service on the importance of wildlife revealed that Canadians, probably Americans as well, placed a high value on wildlife. Each year more than 60 percent of the Canadian population fed, watched, photographed, or provided for wildlife around their homes. This shows that appreciating backyard wildlife is an important recreational pursuit.

The enjoyment of wildlife, like the enjoyment of art, music, or literature, is a creative act. While it can be a matter of passive exposure, it may be enriched many times through active involvement. Through our windows, the world and its wildlife may be fascinating or dull, thrilling or frightening, ugly or beautiful according to our personal perspective. For people who wish to improve their gardens for wildlife, the quality of their experience will depend first on what they "sow" or develop and second on their ability to observe and interpret what they see.

In the past, truly great naturalists such as Charles Darwin and J. H. Fabre, spent decades in their gardens observing, studying, experimenting, and recording observations of plants and wild creatures.

For Fabre, whose career had humble beginnings, there was

one overriding desire. This was how he expressed it in his book The World of Insects.

> This was what I wished for: a bit of land, oh not so very large, but fenced in to avoid the drawbacks of a public way; an abandoned barren, sun scorched bit of land, favoured by thistles and by wasps and bees. Yes, this was my wish, my dream, always cherished, always vanishing into the mists of the future.

Perhaps no other backyard has been more appreciated or has produced more fascinating insights into the habits of insects. For Fabre, natural history was a passion; the writings which sprang from his indulgence are classic.

Few of us might wish a garden favored by thistles, wasps, and bees, but the joys we reap through careful observation could be equally satisfying. But for the backyard wildlife gardener the diversity of animal and plant species we have to work with is both a joy and a headache! The joy comes from the variety of choice, the headache from having to make decisions.

Whatever our situation, local conditions such as climate, elevation, exposure, and soil type will pose some limitations on our desires. Fortunately, most of the plant and animal species we may wish to encourage have wide ranges and broad levels of tolerance. Nonetheless, local knowledge will be very important.

Supplying all this knowledge is beyond the scope of this book. However, rest assured that your community nurseryperson, naturalist, nature center, government agency, and other experts will often provide this information with pleasure. Do not hesitate to seek their advice or assistance. Since many heads are better than one, consulting these people can save you considerable time, effort, and expense.

One last comment is that there is more to wildlife enjoyment than just looking for, and at, birds. This statement is not made to criticize birders and bird enthusiasts. It is made simply to remind us all that there are tremendous rewards and viewing pleasures to be derived from non-avian forms. While many of us think of birds first, let's not overlook those other interesting but perhaps more retiring species.

Before we get into the how, what, when, where, and why of

backyard wildlife gardening, let's take a brief look at four important general considerations. These are: first, an understanding of the "needs" of all wildlife; second, knowing your personal preferences; third, recognizing your garden's unique features; and finally, setting realistic limits on your expectations. With these as your cornerstones, your chances of success will be greatly increased.

THE NEEDS OF ALL WILDLIFE

Simply stated, all wildlife has four basic requirements for survival. The first is sufficient space within which the remaining three—shelter, food, and water—must occur.

The combination of these requirements to ensure survival varies greatly from one species to another, even from one season to the next. No two species, be they chipmunk or squirrel or closely allied species of dragonflies, have identical needs.

Generally speaking, the larger and more diverse an area is in its terrain, variety of habitats and species of plants present; the more species of wildlife and more individuals of a species it can accommodate.

When it comes to backyards of limited extent, most species will be transients. Their presence will only correspond to the ability of the area to meet their specific needs. For this reason, each species will move or shift from one area to another by day or by season. A good example is the tree frog or Spring Peeper, which spends its springs breeding in ponds and the remainder of its active season in nearby foliage. Unless all the tree frog's needs are met in one area, the frog will move to another location. The challenge to the backyard gardener who desires tree frogs year round in his garden is to provide both an attractive pool and suitable surrounding vegetation.

When the general requirements of a species are known, the backyard challenge is to provide these in smaller areas than might be normal. This is the role of enhancement—the enriching of an area beyond its "normal" potential.

CONSIDERATIONS

For Shelter: Shelter takes many forms, including protection from severe weather, availability of safe resting, roosting, and hiding areas, and ample space to successfully rear young. In the normal backyard with limited space, all these cannot be provided. But through careful planning and imaginative design, these can be improved considerably.

For Food: Seasonal changes in natural food supply and individual preferences cause many kinds of wildlife to move from one area to another. These continual shifts in diet and food availability can be overcome in a number of ways. Means to this end include providing additional food supplies either by planting known and preferred food plants that provide a variety of seeds and fruits, developing feeding stations, or attracting food sources such as insects into your area.

For Water: The need for water is possibly the most overlooked and underestimated need of wildlife. Water is important for bathing and for drinking. For many amphibians and insects it is essential for completing their life cycle. If you are fortunate enough to have a natural water source on your property, rejoice! If not, then give serious consideration to developing one. Pools, baths, and seeps all have their place as focal points in a backyard for urban wildlife.

TAKING STOCK

In planning your backyard wildlife area, there are many important questions you ought to ask yourself before you proceed. The following are some of the important ones.

1. What are your backyard wildlife preferences?
   a) butterflies?
   b) song birds?
   c) frogs?
   d) small mammals?
2. Before you buy a lot or property:
   a) How big an area will you have for the garden?
   b) Does the property have a sunny (southerly) exposure?
   c) Does the property have a good and varied selection of trees, shrubs, and native plants?
   d) Does the property have a natural water supply (a spring, pond, or small stream)?
   e) Does the property adjoin a park, woodlot, ravine, or other wild area?

f) Does the property have a varied and interesting topog-
raphy?

3. Do any of your neighbors or potential neighbors share your
interest in backyard wildlife?

4. Do they wish to participate and get involved in improving
their yards as well?

5. Are predators, particularly cats and dogs, going to be a continual nuisance?

6. Are young, noisy children going to present problems?

7. What local regulations are in place regarding property use,
zoning, noxious animals or weeds?

8. Is there a development plan for the neighborhood?

9. What kinds of soil are present and are these conducive to
gardening?

10. Are their any epidemic tree diseases, insect pests, or
noxious weeds apparent in the area?

11. Do the local Authorities or neighbors regularly spray herbicides or insecticides?

If your immediate neighbors share your enthusiasm and interest, encourage their participation to considerably expand you
"effective wildlife area." Ask them. Nothing can be lost and
there is much you could gain!

Unless an area has been bulldozed flat and scraped of all vegetation, every property should have some features which can be
included in your wildlife landscaping plan. Some features to be
cherished include:

dirt piles	ditches
rock piles	pools
boulders	steep slopes
stumps	weed patches
logs	trees and shrubs
snags	

In fact, any landscape feature can be used to advantage.
Trees, in particular deciduous trees and shrubs, should be protected from damage during house construction. If these plants
do not fit readily into your long-term plan, they can prove to be
very helpful while other, more desirable species and plantings
grow to sufficient size and height to take over.

Having considered basic needs of wildlife, and having taken

stock of what your property offers in the way of natural features, you should be in position to second-guess what factor or
factors are limiting wildlife use in your garden.

A limiting factor is an item or need that, by its absence, prevents or regulates greater use by the animal species present. By
providing or improving this factor, you stand to increase the
use of your garden significantly.

What, then, is going to be the one factor in your backyard
that most limits its use by insects, reptiles, amphibians, birds
or mammals? Is it food, shelter, or water? My suspicion would
be that it will be a suitable source of water!

Keeping your personal preferences in mind, and recognizing
the limiting factors, you will find in the following chapters
specific information on what you might like to try and how you
might overcome some of the potential limitations.

TAILORING YOUR EXPECTATIONS

A year ago, a gentleman, quite knowledgeable about wildlife
and natural history, told me how his winter works project had
been the construction of a multi-apartment Purple Martin
house for a children's home in his community. He had labored
on this creation for many evenings over a number of months
and was now about to erect his masterpiece. It was beautiful—
but—there were no Purple Martins in his area. His creation, although attractive, had little practical value. Before he had even
started, he should have asked himself, "What are the common
bird species which nest in this community?" and, "Which ones
will readily use a nest box?"

Armed with this information and for the same effort at less
cost, he could have built a dozen swallow boxes and robin nesting brackets. These would have had the potential of producing
very positive results.

Half the battle in encouraging and improving gardens for
wildlife is knowing what to expect. Once this knowledge is at
hand, matching species, be they bugs, bats, or birds, with their
basic needs, is much easier.

In addition to knowing what species are present, it is also
important to know when they are present, and what their

Plate 1
Shelter from overhanging branches providing a foraging area for ground-feeding birds during snowfalls.

habitat preferences might be. Since many species migrate, hibernate, or are quite selective in habitat, their appearance is often seasonal.

Information on the species in your area and when they are present is not likely to be available in your local library. Most of their books will be more general in scope. Check first with your local museum by asking what they have, and who in your area might have this knowledge.

If there is a naturalist club, Audubon society, or nature center association in your area, its members will supply you with information. Your local tourist bureau or recreation commission should have the club's address or even know some of its members. Government employees concerned with fish, wildlife, or parks might also be able to help.

The following chapters give some ideas and list some common species you might expect to find in your area. To avoid disappointment, know what to expect.

Plate 2
A natural water source improved by a short length of plastic pipe.

Plate 3
A snag designated for use by wildlife by the British Columbia Fish and Wildlife Branch.

2

Gardens for Butterflies and Bugs

Of all backyard wildlife, insects and spiders are the least un-
derstood, most overlooked or neglected, and yet are
among the most fascinating. To appreciate insects and spiders
and to observe their intricate habits requires patience and skill.
Remember, sight is a faculty, but seeing is an art!

Insects in northern areas are primarily warm season wildlife.
Of the thousands of species present, we can look at only a very
few of the common groups. These, of necessity, must be the
large, showy, easily identified, and numerous forms, common
to most gardens. The right conditions will bring all these
species, wanted or unwanted, into the average garden.

No plant is totally immune to the ravages of insects, be they
the nibblers, suckers, chewers, hunters or simply resters.
Often more than one stage of an insect's life cycle will be present. This is especially true of moths, butterflies, and aquatic
forms, where both adults and their larvae are likely to frequent
the same plant or pool.

Insects and spiders are also the prime food of countless other
insects, reptiles and amphibians, birds, and small mammals.
Because of their importance in the food chain, having a really
bug-infested yard can have its advantages! For those people

TABLE 2.1
COMMON BACKYARD INSECTS AND SPIDERS

Insect Types	General Needs	Interesting Characteristics
Dragonflies	Open areas near pools with emergent vegetation	Noisy, colorful fliers, help control mosquitoes and black flies
Damselflies	Pool with emergent vegetation	Dainty and colourful, also eat Mosquitoes
Grasshoppers	Sunny, grassy location	Aerial noisemakers on hot days. Some may damage garden plants.
Crickets	Sunny location with loose cover	Chorus on warm summer evenings
Ladybird Beetles	Sunny garden	Colorful adults—adults and larvae feed on aphids and scale insects
Butterflies	Nectar-rich flowers, moisture and appropriate plants for larval development	Bright, colorful fliers
Moths	Night blooming flowers	Large species most attractive. Sphinx Moth flies like hummingbird
Hover Flies	Open, sunny area with flowers	Mimic bees and wasps in size, shape, color, and noise, but are harmless—larvae feed on aphids
Ants	Cracks in wall or flag stones	Colonial workers with flying adults
Bumble Bees	Flowers—will nest in nest boxes	Large, colorful buzzers. They can but seldom sting
Hornets, Yellowjackets	Dry overhang	Paper-making—sting may produce allergic reaction
Orb Spiders	Shrubbery	Large webs as insect traps
Wolf Spiders	Sunny, vegetated area near a wall	Females carry a large egg case on their backs

TABLE 2.2
SOME NATIVE PLANTS ATTRACTIVE TO INSECTS

Species	Flowering Season	Insects
Willow, *Salix* species	Early spring	Aphids, moths, ants, Tiger Swallowtail
Spirea, *Spiraea species*	Late spring to early summer	Bees
Wild Rose, *Rosa* species	Early summer	Bees
Cow Parsnip, *Heracleum* species	Early summer	Flies, long-horned beetles
Blue Elderberry, *Sambucus cerulea*	Late spring through summer	Flies
Dandelion, *Taraxacum* species	Early spring	Bees, syrphid flies, Crab Spiders
Pearly-everlasting, *Anaphalis margaritacea*	Summer	Syrphid flies, bees, skippers, butterflies
Dogbane *Apocynum* species	Summer	Butterflies
Thistles, *Cirsium* species	Summer	Bumble bees, Painted Lady Butterfly
Milkweeds, *Asclepias* species	Summer	Monarch Butterfly
Goldenrod *Solidago* species	Late summer into autumn	Syrphid flies, skippers, butterflies
Asters and Michaelmas-Daisy, *Aster* species	Late summer into autumn	Bees, flies, butterflies

who wish to appreciate backyard wildlife in its broadest sense, insects offer a challenge not easily dismissed.

A lesson that many organic gardeners understand well is that many interesting insects actually control some of the pest species. The best example is the Ladybird Beetle (Ladybug), which feeds on aphids. Some gardeners actually import these predatory species for this purpose.

In this chapter we will look at three broad concepts: the development of a garden for butterflies, the importance of a good pool for aquatic insects, and some ideas for attracting "dry land" groups such as bees, grasshoppers, crickets, and spiders.

Some common groups of backyard insects, their needs and interesting characteristics are listed in Table 2.1. Tables 2.2 and 2.3 provide some ideas about the species of native and horticultural plants that are attractive to these insects.

TABLE 2.3
SOME HORTICULTURAL PLANTS ATTRACTIVE TO INSECTS

Species	Comments
Horsechestnut
Aesculus species	Also attractive to hummingbirds
(pink-flowering variety)
Butterfly Bush
Buddleia davidii	Vigorous—grows like a weed. Very
attractive to butterflies.
Lilac
Syringa species	Attractive to butterflies and
clear-winged moths.
Weigela
Weigela species and varieties	A bumble bee favorite
Heath
Erica species	Attractive to bees
Cotoneaster
Cotoneaster species and varieties	Flowers in spring, berries in fall and
winter (Birds)
Tower of Jewels
Echium wildprettii	An interesting oddity, attractive to
bees
Hops
Humulus lupulus	Attractive to many insect types.
Grows quickly
Red Clover
Trifolium pratense	A bumble bee favorite

THE BUTTERFLY GARDEN

The requirements for a butterfly garden are quite simple, and are virtually no different, except by degree, from those required for any other wildlife species.

First is a sunny location protected from prevailing winds, with ample sites for resting and sunning.

TABLE 2.4
COMMON BUTTERFLIES AND THEIR LARVAL FOOD PLANTS

Species	Larval Plant	
Monarch	Milkweed	*Asclepasis* species
Danaus plexippus	Dogbane	*Apocynum* species
Swallowtails	Cow parsnip	*Heracleum* species
Papilio species	Spring gold and Biscuit-roots	*Lomatium* species
	Fennel	*Foeniculum vulgare*
	Dill	*Anethum graveolens*
Tiger Swallowtail,	Cottonwood	*Populus* species
Papilio species	Wild Cherry	*Prunus* species
	Willow	*Salix* species
	Maple	*Acer* species
	Alder	*Alnus* species
Cabbage White,	Cabbage and Mustard	Vegetable garden varieties
Pieris rapae	Nasturtium	*Tropaeolum majus*
Sulphurs	Sweet-clover	*Melilotus* species
Colias species	Clovers	*Trifolim* species
Mourning Cloak,	Willow	*Salix* species
Nymphalis antiopa	Cottonwood	*Populus* species
Painted Lady,	Thistle	*Cirsium* species
Cynthia cardui	Pearly-everlasting	*Anaphalis margaritacea*
Red Admiral,	Stinging Nettle	*Urtica dioica*
Vanessa atalanta	Hops	*Humulus lupulus*
Lorquin's Admiral,	Willow	*Salix* species
Basilarchia lorquini,	Cottonwood	*Populus* species
White Admiral,	Cherry	*Prunus* species
Basilarchia arthemis	Spirea	*Spiraea* species
	Apple	*Pyrus* species
Skippers, a variety of species	Grasses—many types	

The second requirement is a profusion, both in numbers and variety, of sweet scented and colorful flowers. Select flowers to ensure a flowering progression from early spring until late autumn. Note: many popular cultivated flowers have lost their aroma during horticultural development. Check this feature carefully! Some good butterfly plants for the garden include the penstemons (*Penstemon* species), the columbines (*Aquilegia* species), the jewelweeds (*Impatiens* species), and many of the plants in Tables 2.2, 2.3, 2.4, and 4.4.

In addition to nectar producing flowers, adult butterflies also require special plants on which to lay their eggs. A list of some common butterfly species and their larval food plants is included in Table 2.4. With these plants present the butterfly's life cycle can be completed in your garden (Figure 2.1).

While most butterflies will obtain the water they require from the flowers they visit, many species seem to enjoy a damp area from which to drink. This requirement can be provided as a "seep". A seep is simply an area that is kept moist by a small but constant supply of water. A shallow pool edge filled with coarse sand or the overflow from a bird bath or an air conditioner are three possible water sources.

In addition to flowers, some butterflies (wasps and moths too) are attracted to rotting fruit, particularly apples. Some species can even be baited to an area by supplying a mixture of ingredients listed below.

A RECIPE FOR A BUTTERFLY OR MOTH BAIT

Ingredients:
- 1 litre low alcohol beer
- 450 grams brown sugar
- 1 tablespoon rum
- 1 tablespoon honey
- 1 slice brown bread
- 1 apple (cut into small pieces and dried)

Procedure:
Mix ingredients together and let stand for 12 -24 hours.

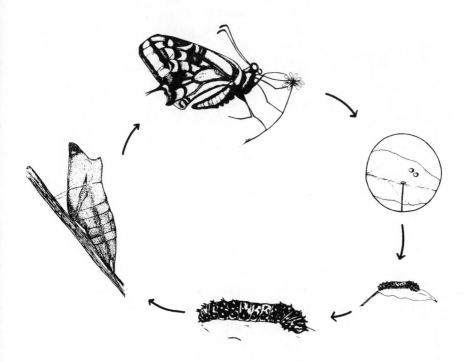

Figure 2.1
Life cycle of the Anise Swallowtail.

To set out bait, take pieces of 5 cm (2 in.) thick sponge and cut into squares 8 cm x 8 cm (3 in. x 3 in.). Soak these in the solution and tie them with string to trees, posts, etc.

The large, strikingly colored species or moths, including the sphinx and hawk moths, *Cecropia, Luna,* and *Polyphemus* are much more numerous than generally believed. Night flowering plants such as the Evening Primrose (*Oenothera* species) will attract Sphinx moths, which feed from these flowers - hummingbird fashion. Watching them feed is a wonderful experience. An outside light, such as illustrated for bats in Figure 3.5, will often attract the other species mentioned above.

One last, and perhaps the most important consideration for a successful butterfly garden: your garden must be a *pesticide-free* zone.

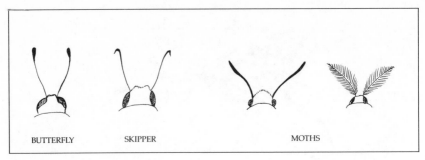

BUTTERFLY   SKIPPER   MOTHS

Figure 2.2
Antennae - telling butterflies from skippers and moths.

A POND FOR BACKYARD INSECTS

Because ponds provide a permanent water source they add an important dimension in diversity to the average garden. Just about all animal species will benefit in some way from a pool, but flying aquatic insects will benefit most. In fact, many of the showier species such as damselflies and dragonflies may develop through their entire life cycle (Figure 2.3) in or near a small pool. Even the pesky, despised mosquito, with its multiform life cycle (Figure 2.4) can easily, when unmolested, pass from egg to adult and to egg again, in the smallest pool, or indeed, a cup of water!

The garden pond may range in size from a bathtub sunk into the corner of a garden, to a mammoth concrete structure, carefully contoured to fit the natural terrain. Whatever the size and shape, when artistically planted with local marsh plants, the garden pool can be extremely attractive.

A good pool or pond for wildlife should contain areas with different water depths to support a variety of aquatic plants (Figure 2.5). Shallow areas with gently sloping beaches are especially desirable (see Plate 4A).

While it may take a year or two, eventually a balanced system will emerge in a newly planted pond.

A general rule of thumb to help determine the number of plants required for your pond is one water lily and three bunches of green pond weeds per square meter of pond surface. Green pond weeds include the Canada Water Weed (*Elodea*

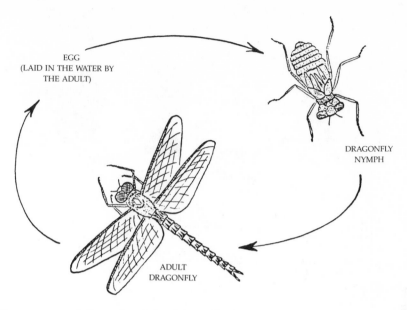

EGG
(LAID IN THE WATER BY
THE ADULT)

DRAGONFLY
NYMPH

ADULT
DRAGONFLY

Figure 2.3   *Life cycle of the dragonfly.*

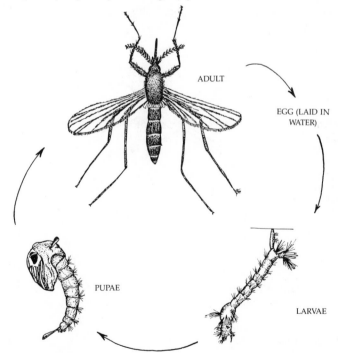

ADULT

EGG (LAID IN
WATER)

PUPAE

LARVAE

Figure 2.4   *Mosquito life cycle.*

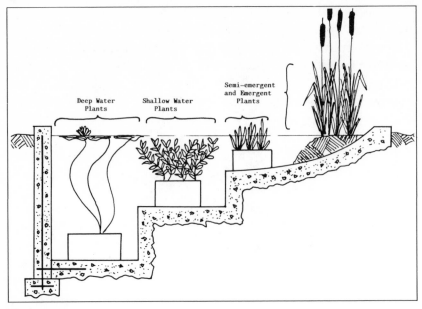

Figure 2.5
Cross section of a concrete pool showing different water depths for a variety of aquatic plants.

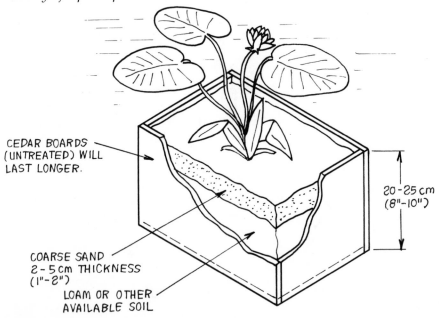

Figure 2.6
A method of planting aquatic plants in an outdoor pool.

canadensis), the Pondweeds, (*Potamogeton* species), and the native Water Milfoils (*Myriophyllum* species).

Successfully transplanting water plants from a wild pond to a garden pool is usually fairly easy. Some species such as the attractive Water Shield (*Brasenia schreberi*) are more difficult and have special requirements for water quality. Trial and error will distinguish those species that survive from those that perish.

To prevent widespread or invasive species from overrunning your pool, confine them in large pots or boxes. To prevent the soil from clouding the water, cover the bare soil and roots with a thin layer of coarse, clean sand (Figure 2.6).

Some common native plants worthy of introduction to the backyard pond are listed in Table 2.5. Don't be afraid to experiment with other species whose natural growing conditions you feel able to duplicate.

TABLE 2.5
SOME COMMON NATIVE PLANTS SUITABLE FOR THE BACKYARD POOL

Floating Plants	Duckweed	*Lemna minor*
	Bladderwort	*Utricularia vulgaris*
Deep Water 50–150 cm deep	Yellow Waterlily	*Nuphar lutea*
	Canada Waterweed	*Elodea canadensis*
	Watershield	*Brasenia schreberi*
	Water-milfoil	*Myriophyllum* species
	Pondweeds	*Potamogeton* species
Shallow Water semi-emergent species 5–15 cm deep	Cattail	*Typha latifolia*
	Yellow Iris	*Iris pseudacrous*
	Arrowhead	*Sagittaria* species
	Waterplantain	*Alisma plantago-aquatica*
	Buckbean	*Menyanthes trifoliata*
	Rush	*Juncus* species
	Marsh Cinquefoil	*Potentilla palustris*
Emergent and Shoreline Plants	Douglas's Spirea	*Spiraea douglasii*
	Meadow Sweet	*Spiraea alba*
	Sweet Gale	*Myrica gale*
	Willow	*Salix* species
	Loosestrife	*Lythrum salicaria*
	Skullcap	*Scutellaria* species
	Water-parsley	*Oenanthe sarmentosa*
	Small-flowered Forget-me-not	*Myosotis laxa*
	Blue Iris	*Iris* species

CARE AND MAINTENANCE OF THE GARDEN POOL

Once a pond and its plant life become a balanced unit, annual care and maintenance should be minimal. Each spring and/or fall the removal of excess organic matter such as fallen leaves, needles, and dead stalks of the previous season's growth will prolong the period between major cleanings.

Loss of clarity in ponds often indicates that something is out of balance. Excessive amounts of dead vegetation or the presence of garden fertilizers are often the primary problem. This can be corrected by removing or reducing the sources when known, or by replacing the fouled water with clean.

Remember: Tap water, especially in summer, is often laced with chlorine. Use rain water from a nearby roof, or water from a natural source whenever possible.

If you must use tap water, let it stand for thirty-six to forty-eight hours before returning any animals to your pool. This will allow any chlorine present to evaporate.

Pools and ponds with fish, frogs, or tadpoles are common attractions for curious children. Never forget public safety when young children are about.

CONSTRUCTING A BACKYARD POOL

There are at least four types of pools you may wish to consider for your garden. The first takes advantage of your local situation. If you are fortunate to have a low damp hollow where the water table is close to the surface, a simple pond, dug to the shape, size, and depth you desire, may suffice. This will fill naturally with ground water, and with a little artistic licence can be made very attractive. Depending on depth and the nature of the soil, sloughing and caving in of the pool's bank could be a problem. During dry periods your pool could go dry. In other situations where natural ground water is not available, pools can be built using a variety of materials. One method utilizes poly vinyl chloride (PVC) as a plastic liner, a second uses cement, shaped and formed to your imagination. Some companies produce molded fibreglass pools which only need to be sunk in place, and some people, possibly a little less discriminating (but thrifty), use an old sink, bathtub, or similar object destined for the local dump. Whatever the type or source, each can be made very attractive. For wildlife the concrete pool is perhaps best because the texture of the cement provides a non-skid surface.

BUILDING A PVC POOL

Poly vinyl chloride is a strong, somewhat elastic, plastic material which can stretch with ice pressure and earth settling. Not to be confused with polyethylene, which hardens and cracks with age, PVC keeps its original properties and is said to last as long as concrete.

PVC pool liners come in a variety of sizes up to 5.5 x 7.5 m (18 x 25 ft.). These liners are less expensive than concrete and do not require the heavy labor of mixing and pouring cement. All you need do is dig the hole to the required size and shape, smooth out the bottom and sides to remove any sharp objects, then lay in the liner and fill your new pool. Some effort will be required to touch up the pool rim to hide the edges of the liner.

For further information on this type of pool, contact a nursery specializing in water gardens.

BUILDING A CONCRETE POOL

Constructing a concrete pool is not as easy as it first may appear. Since a cubic meter of wet cement weighs about 2000 kg (2¼ tons), expect some heavy work, even if you plan to use ready-mix delivered by truck!

Depending on location, you may be forced to build a free form pool that uses local features and contours. These more natural pools can quite easily be tucked into a chosen location to fit neatly with your garden plan. Because wet cement flows readily, it may be difficult to provide sufficient depth in the center of a small pond to meet the needs of some aquatic plants, especially water lilies. In these circumstances, rock walls or other barriers to increase the pool's gradient may be needed. You may wish to construct these barriers over a period of time. In all cases, a depth of at least 75 cm (30 in.), and preferably 100 cm (40 in.), should be minimal.

A second type of concrete pool is the *formed pool*, that utilizes ordinary builders' cement forms into which the wet cement is poured. These forms and their attendant hardware are best rented, and they are quick and easy to set up. Pools built with these forms have vertical walls of geometric shape unless special steps are taken to alter this configuration.

In the construction of a good pool which can be used easily by wildlife, components of both types of construction are desirable. While vertical walls provide greater depth, shallow embankments allow for diversity. If, when building your pool, you use imagination for its shape, form, and materials, your creation can be both practical and aesthetically pleasing.

Some General Specifications for a Formed Pool (Figure 2.7)

Either the floor or footings to support the wall should be poured first. Because pools are likely to freeze in winter, 15 mm (½ in.) steel reinforcing bars should be used both horizontally and vertically at about 50 cm (20 in.) intervals to prevent or reduce cracking.

To ensure a snug fit between the walls and either the floor or footing, a key or depression should be made to provide a good joint.

Remember: Never underestimate the strength of wet cement. If your forms break you are in for a terrible amount of grief. Should you have any concerns or hesitation, consult or obtain advice from a local contractor or cement expert. They may provide you with many good ideas which could make your job easier and your pool more attractive.

Curing Your Pool

Free lime that leaches from new concrete is quite toxic to plants, fish, and aquatic insects. Filling and flushing your new pool three or four times at intervals of at least twenty-four hours will remove most of the lime. On the last rinse let the water stand for a week. Then it should be safe.

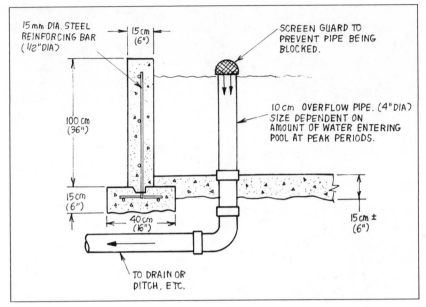

Figure 2.7
Some construction details for a formed concrete pool.

WATER SOURCES FOR YOUR POOL

Exceedingly lucky will be the home owner with a natural spring or small watercourse on his or her property. More likely it will be the garden hose that provides water to your pool. Don't forget, your household roof is a natural water catchment, and by simply directing one of your downpipes to your pool, it could provide all the water you need.

PROVIDING FOR OVERFLOW AND DRAINAGE

To keep your pool from overflowing into your garden, instal a good drainage system as indicated in Figure 2.7. The pipe, cut to the desired length, should friction-fit into the appropriate coupling cemented into the pool's floor. In turn, this exit may lead to a local ditch or your domestic drainage system. To prevent this overflow pipe from becoming plugged, fit the opening with a screen cap as indicated.

Plates 4A & 4B
The author's backyard pool before and after, showing features il-
lustrated in Figure 2.5. All plants were transplanted from nearby
sources.

ENCOURAGING THE DRYLAND INSECTS

The sunny warm days of spring, and even more so, the hot days of summer are the times when terrestrial insects are most active. From the great flights of large, black carpenter ants during May, to the fall chorus of field crickets, we have a considerable richness of insect events. Because of this richness, the number of opportunities the backyard gardener may cultivate is virtually endless. Some, like the grasshopper or aphid, may be unwanted. Nonetheless, each has its place in our environment. We can observe all of them, and from each, we can learn.

Here are some thoughts and ideas about a wide range of insects that require a dry, warm, sunny niche. Water is often not an important consideration, as many get the moisture they need from the foods they eat. Others will appreciate a source of free water.

Grasshoppers

These long-legged jumpers, well known to most of us, come in a variety of shapes and colors. Some, like the katydids and meadow grasshoppers, may be bright green in color. Most, however, are combinations of grey and brown.

After hatching, the development of this group could be characterized as one of growth and moult. Unlike the mosquito or dragonfly, the first hatchling looks very much like a diminutive adult (Figure 2.8).

The most noticeable species are the larger members of the short-horned grasshopper group. Their wings often show flashes of red or yellow during their noisy, snapping flight. Semi-arid patches of dry, warm ground seem to be the preferred take-off points for these flights. In a garden setting these could be a bank, children's play area, or even an unpaved driveway.

Crickets

Field crickets are close cousins to the grasshoppers. These are the shiny black crickets found under loose objects, and inside cracks and crevices (Plate 5). On warm summer evenings the songs of these animals produce a pleasant chorus.

Plate 5
A male Field cricket.

Females are easily separated from the males by their long, straight ovipositor (resembling a straight pin) that projects about 2 cm (.8 in.) from the rear of the abdomen.

A warm dry area with lots of hiding places is an ideal environment for field crickets.

Ladybird Beetles (Lady Bugs)

Ketchup-red with black spots, these small beetles are harbingers of joy. Most every small child, with a ladybird perched on his or her finger, has recited the verse,

> Ladybird, Ladybird
> Fly away home.
> Your house is on fire
> And your children are alone.

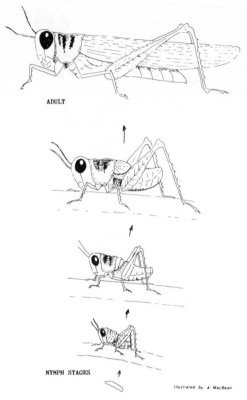

ADULT

NYMPH STAGES

Illustrated by A. MacBean

Figure 2.8
Life cycle of a short-horned grasshopper.

As often as not, the tiny little beetle then spreads its wings and flies off!

Though universally present in small numbers, the adults sometimes overwinter in large groups of many thousands.

It is not easy to encourage ladybirds to frequent your garden. However, their presence should be appreciated as both adults and larvae are important predators of aphids, scale insects, and mites. Sometimes they are available for purchase from organic gardening suppliers.

Syrphid Flies

Among the great diversity of flies (more than 16,000 species in North America alone) is a group of largish individuals, strikingly patterned in yellow, black, and brown. Most species in this group resemble wasps and bees in their color patterns and even in their behavior. Some, when trapped, even buzz.

These are the hover or syrphid flies. While their appearance and behavior strongly suggest bees, syrphid flies do not sting.

Different species of these flies will be found in every garden, particularly around flowers. Michaelmas-daisy and pearly ever-lasting are two of the better species to attract these flies.

Ants

Ants are colonial, social insects found almost everywhere. Their colonies range in size from a few dozen to many thou-sands of individuals. Together they build or occupy a nest which may occupy a crack in a wall or a cavity under a boulder. Sometimes they will pull together a large pile of vegetation over several years. The thatching ant (*Formica rufa*) may build nests a meter (39 in.) high and 4 - 5 m (13 - 17 ft.) in circumference.

Owing to this group's wide distribution it will be the excep-tional garden that does not have an ant colony somewhere. As long as it is not an active colony of carpenter ants in the wall or floor of your house, enjoy their presence. Although some may bite, they are generally harmless. The garden peony requires ants for pollination.

One of the interesting events in the ant's annual cycle is a dispersal flight of fertile males and queens. These winged forms depart from their home colony in spring and early sum-mer. From large nests these potential progenitors of new colonies erupt skyward like smoke from a smoldering fire. This event may take place over several weeks, depending on weather conditions.

Bumble Bees

These fuzzy creatures, strikingly marked with black, orange, white, and yellow, are found widely. Like their relative the honeybee, bumble bees can be induced to nest in boxes (Figure 2.9), similar to those we build for cavity nesting birds. In fact, these bees occasionally take over nest sites being used by chickadees and creepers.

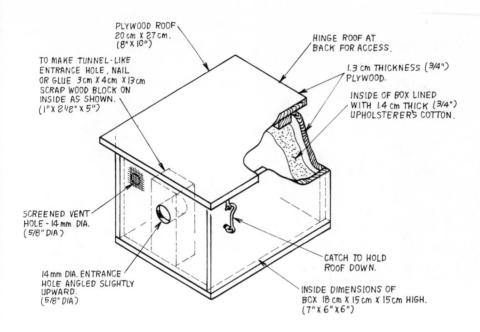

Figure 2.9
Construction details of a Bumblebee nest box.

Yellowjackets and Hornets

These are the pesky wasps that occasionally disrupt our summer picnics and barbecues. Though easily maligned during these times, wasps are not without their merit. As producers of paper, they are without equal.

For the patient and not easily perturbed observer, the papermaking process is easily observed at nest sites being constructed by a solitary queen. Rough, weathered wood placed near the queen's construction site will often be used as the source of pulp. Since the queen is the only individual to winter over, this process must be observed early in the season before the colony grows. As long as the observer remains quiet, the wasp's work will continue in comparative safety to both parties.

Plate 6   *A large nest of the Bald-faced Hornet. Interesting to watch from a safe distance with binoculars.*

Plate 8   *An Orb spider web anchored to long grass.*

Plate 7   *The edge of a concrete wall with long grass. A great place for crickets and wolf spiders.*

Plate 9   *Pearly Everlasting flowers, a favourite of bees, flies and butterflies as a food and nectar source.*

Both the yellowjacket and the hornet are voracious predators of other insects. There is also no honor among species, as the larger hornets often attack and dismember their smaller cousins.

If wasps are a problem see Chapter 11, Eliminating Wasps.

Mud-Dauber Wasps

These large, handsome wasps are very partial to damp locations where mud is available. Most of the strikingly marked mud-daubers are shiny, blue-black, and yellow; others are brown and yellow. All have a long 'thread waist'. Their nesting chambers are built of mud in cracks or crevices. These cells are provisioned with spiders on which the young mud-daubers will feed. Providing a source of mud will attract this common wasp.

Spiders

Spiders are perhaps the most fascinating of all the terrestrial arthropods. Their popularity is attested in a number of popular books and countless articles that expose their varied lives.

The most familiar species common to most gardens will be the orb-weaving spiders. These build the large circular webs commonly seen during autumn and appreciated most when the web is laced with dew on a bright morning.

A second group of web builders is the dome weavers. Their dome-like structures are much finer and more elaborate, reflecting the daintiness of the builder.

The spiders found around the grassy borders of our gardens and along our walls are most likely wolf spiders. In spring the female carries an aspirin-sized egg sack on her back until the young spiderlings hatch.

Two additional groups of spiders to look for include crab spiders and jumping spiders. Crab spiders are white to yellow, often with a short, red stripe along each side of the abdomen. They hide in flowers waiting for their prey.

Jumping spiders are attractive, active, little spiders, strikingly patterned with grey, white, black, or orange markings. Their gait is irregular and often they jump. Jumping spiders have eight eyes, which gives them good vision.

Around the garden they are found in bright sunny areas near cracks and crevices.

All our spiders are predators, but none of our common garden spiders are harmful. In undisturbed areas, the poisonous Northern Widow, closely allied to the Black Widow, may occur. Both species are shiny black, and have the red hourglass marking on their abdomen.

To encourage spiders, be sure to provide sites for their webs, such as tangles of longish vegetation against walks and fences.

3

Gardens for Small Mammals, Reptiles, and Amphibians

Years ago, a house we purchased came complete with a large, active colony of carpenter ants, which was munching its way through the timbers behind the kitchen sink. These ants had their access or exit on the outside near the sill. From this opening, they made forays into the garden to quench their thirst. The noise was obvious and somewhat perturbing, but due to the magnitude of the problem and difficulty of repair, not to mention a personal prejudice against chemical extermination, procrastination was the order of the day.

As spring passed into summer, the ants' activity, rather than increasing, began to diminish. Along the nearby footpath, we began to find small scats tightly packed with second-hand ant skeletons. Thank goodness none of us stumbled upon the animal responsible, but the skunk or family of skunks present provided enough biological control that eventually the once-thriving colony foundered and was never again a problem.

This solution was an unexpected and educational sidelight to the enjoyment of rural, backyard wildlife. Would it not be nice if all problems with cohabiting wildlife could be solved by simple inaction!

Providing for small mammals, reptiles, and amphibians in a backyard setting is a frustrating challenge. For three main reasons the chances of reward for effort are not high. First, small mammals and amphibians are often nocturnal. Second, they are quite secretive, and lastly, due to their size and habits, they are often the first species to fall prey to local cats and dogs.

Around feeding stations, the surplus or scattered food from daytime users easily becomes a prime attraction to unwanted rats and mice. This becomes a real problem when enhancement practices to encourage desirable species bring in the unwanted.

Taking these considerations into account, it will be the exceptional rather than the average backyard that can cater to reptiles and amphibians and small mammals. Therefore, your efforts to encourage the desirable species must consider the problem of neighborhood predators and the undesirable presence of introduced rats and mice.

Tables 3.1 and 3.2 list some of the common species likely to be found in many gardens. Also listed are some of their needs and interesting habits.

TABLE 3.1
COMMON BACKYARD SMALL MAMMALS

Species	Needs	Interesting Characteristics
Deer Mouse White-footed Mouse	edges, beaches, logs, brush piles vacant buildings	twilight scamperers
Red Squirrel, Douglas Squirrel	coniferous trees with aerial highways, nearby seed source	aerial acrobats, noisy chatterers
Gray Squirrel, Fox Squirrel	nut trees large hardwood trees	often travel along telephone cables, can be a real garden pest
Flying Squirrel	mature forest areas, use nest boxes as daytime hideaways	night gliders, quiet
Chipmunks	sunny areas with rock piles, logs, and lots of hiding places; nearby seed and berry sources; protection from predators	daytime gatherers
Raccoon	daytime shelter, water to "wash" food	omnivorous, masked evening scroungers
Striped Skunk	denning areas	nocturnal scavenger, often present in cities
Bats (many species)	roosting areas, flying insect food source	nocturnal aerial acrobats

TABLE 3.2
COMMON BACKYARD REPTILES AND AMPHIBIANS

Species	Needs	Interesting Characteristics
AMPHIBIANS		
Pacific Treefrog *Hyla regilla* Spring Peeper *Hyla crucifer*	Marshy pond with emergent vegetation	Noisy springtime chorus, often bright green in color, our most common tadpoles
Bullfrog *Rana catesbeiana*	Fairly large ponds with permanent water	Large size, often jump from bank into ponds, large tadpoles, deep jug-o-rum and br-umm calls in spring
Western Toad *Bufo boreas* American Toad *Bufo americanus* Woodhouse's Toad *Bufo woodhousei*	Cool daytime shelter, loose soils, insect food source	Frequent gardens at night, feed on large insects, will forage under night lights
Long-toed Salamander *Ambystoma macrodactylum*	Moist environment with loose litter, pools with cool, clear water	Lays eggs in pools during early spring, larval development and metamorphosis
Rough-skinned Newt *Tariche granulosa* Eastern Newt *Notophthalmus viridescens*	Moist environment with quiet vegetated pools	Bright orange "tummy" with poisonous skin secretion, eastern species spotted
Tiger Salamander *Ambystoma tigrinum*	Ponds without fish	Large size with yellow and black "tiger" markings
Garter Snakes *Thamnophis* species	Sunny exposed banks and garden edges, enjoy water sources	Feed on slugs
Painted Turtle *Chrysemys picta*	Deep pools with muddy bottom, sunning log	Bright scarlet, yellow, and black "tummy" markings
Western Fence Lizard *Sceloporus occidentalis*	Sunny exposed banks with dead branches	An active warm weather lizard
Northern Alligator Lizard *Gerrhonotus coeruleus*	Sunny rocky areas with lots of cracks and fissures	Enjoy sun bathing
Skinks *Eumeces* species	Sunny areas with leaf litter, logs, and rocks	Bright, shiny striped lizards; young have bright blue tails

SMALL MAMMALS

Almost all the small mammals, except possibly the chipmunks and squirrels, tend to be quite secretive. Some, like the Gray Squirrel, have become an integral part of our urban environment where large trees, especially seed producing hardwoods, are present. Planting maples, oaks, hazelnut, saskatoons, and garden corn will attract many of the mammal species into your garden. Feeders that provide these delicacies can also be used.

Nesting boxes, placed on or near the ground for mice and chipmunks and in trees for squirrels can be important daytime retreats. Snags with large hollows and cavities also serve this purpose.

From dusk until dawn is the time the nighttime creatures are active. A special effort will be required if you wish to attract and observe these species.

About Squirrels

To the bird feeding enthusiast squirrels may bring either joy or a severe headache. Like the Steller's Jay and Chickadees, squirrels can be persistent hoarders, carrying away more groceries than they can ever eat. Further, their climbing, jumping, and evasive abilities make them very difficult to outwit.

The Gray Squirrel (with both black and gray color phases) is now established in many of our suburban areas. Where it reaches forested areas in the Northwest it competes with the Douglas Squirrel, with its orange belly, and possibly the white bellied Red Squirrel. All three species can be attracted to backyards stocked with foods such as peanuts or peanut hearts. If nothing else is available, any cereal grain may be targeted.

Keeping squirrels away from bird feeders can be a problem. Sections in Chapter 11 cover squirrel-proofing. One method you may wish to try to minimize conflicts is to provide squirrel foods at a special location, then squirrel-proof the remaining birdfeeders as best you can.

Denning boxes for squirrels can also be provided (Figure 3.1). Even a length of car tire, modified for the purpose can be successful Figure 3.2).

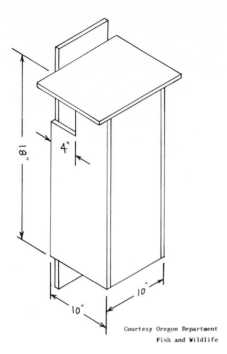

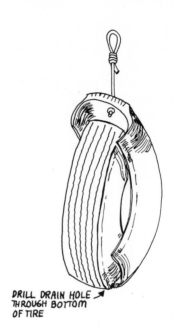

Courtesy Oregon Department
Fish and Wildlife

DRILL DRAIN HOLE
THROUGH BOTTOM
OF TIRE

Figure 3.1
*Rough dimensions and form
for a squirrel nest box.*

Figure 3.2
*A section of a car tire modified
to become a squirrel home.*

About Chipmunks

Chipmunks are the darlings of the rodent world. Though highly desirable as inhabitants of our gardens, their habit of wandering large distances when gathering food exposes them to many predators, particularly domestic cats. For this reason, their survival rate is greatly reduced in urban areas.

In rural areas, fairly open forest and shrub edges with lots of cover provide ideal chipmunk habitat. In spring, chipmunks feed on green leaves and shoots until seeds become plentiful. Occasionally, they also eat insects, flowers, fruits, mushrooms, and birds' eggs. In the Pacific Northwest chipmunks show a particular affinity for saskatoon shrubs (*Amelanchier alnifolia*).

A large, flat boulder with dense, nearby shrubbery well supplied with seeds makes an ideal chipmunk feeding table. Sunflower seeds are a favorite.

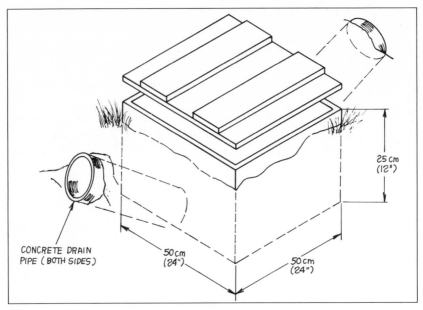

Figure 3.3
An artificial underground burrow for rabbits and hares.

ARTIFICIAL BURROWS FOR TERRESTRIAL MAMMALS

In the wild, rabbits, hares, skunks, and even Burrowing Owls use old burrows for refuge and shelter. Badgers, ground squirrels, and marmots are often the natural providers of these retreats. In areas where natural holes are scarce, artificial burrows made of rough untreated wood and concrete drain tiles (Figure 3.3) can be provided as substitutes. These, fitted with a lid but no bottom, can be partially or totally buried in areas where there is good drainage. To enhance their natural appearance, the lids may be covered with soil, rocks, sod, or brush. Placing these in close proximity to a bank, hedgerow, or other shrubbery will increase use.

CREATURES OF THE NIGHT

Ever since the dawn of time man has feared creatures of the night. As ancient men huddled around their campfires, they heard strange squeaks, hoots, and howls. What man could not see, he invented stories to explain. Much of this early prejudice remains to the present day.

As darkness descends over our gardens, the day shift animals retreat and the night shift begin their appointed rounds. Owls, raccoons, deer mice, toads, bats, and flying squirrels are among this platoon. Most we will never see unless we make a special effort. Although man is not noted for keen night vision, it is surprising just what we can see with only a faint light. For those backyard gardeners with a yen to see nighttime creatures, an electric light placed in an advantageous position will throw light into the darkest corners of the yard. By turning off your inside lights, you greatly improve the chances of seeing night animals entering your area.

Flying Squirrels enjoy sunflower seeds and peanut butter, raccoons a raw egg. Placing a feeding station for these animals in a fairly open position will allow you a regular glimpse.

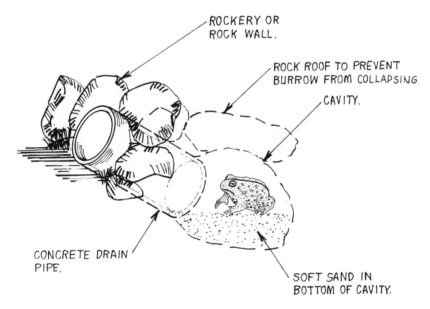

Figure 3.4
Construction details of a toad hole.

About Toads

Toads, either the Western or American, are found throughout the west. While not strictly nocturnal, toads usually emerge from their hiding places to forage at night. Our toads breed in shallow water usually with a sandy bottom. Their eggs, laid in long strings, hatch into black tadpoles (which separates them from frog tadpoles, which are brown). Once hatched, these tadpoles often form large schools that move around the shores of large ponds and lakes.

Toad Holes and Toad Lights

Two ideas for improving backyards for toads are providing daytime retreats and hiding places (Figure 3.4) and a low power light source to attract night insects (Figure 3.5). Toad holes can be constructed in many imaginative ways, with soft sandy soil at the bottom being the key. Such structures can easily be built into a rockery or similar area.

Toad lights may be a light designed to illuminate a foot path. If the light is placed near a border between a garden or rockery and a lawn area, toads will have some cover while waiting for their meal to arrive.

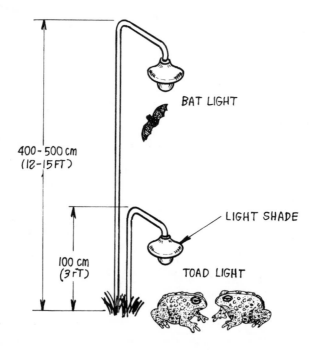

Figure 3.5
Simple light sources to attract insects for toads and bats.

Plates 10A & B
A Northern Flying Squirrel. Note the telltale teethmarks around the entrance to its nest box (right).

About Deer Mice

Deer mice delight in scampering about quiet locations just after dark. With large ears, large eyes, and long tails they are quite distinct from the Meadow Mouse or introduced House Mouse.

Though deer mice are numerous, they are difficult to observe. If you want a good close look, use a live trap baited with peanut butter. Sometimes deer mice will enter a lighted room or cabin provided all is still and quiet.

Dry hollows in stumps, walls, or attics are preferred locations for nest sites and daytime retreats. Often they build their bulky nests in a bluebird-size nest box that is placed close to the ground and partially screened by vegetation. Boxes for these purposes should have a second exit at one of the top rear corners.

Deer mice are omnivorous, feeding on a wide variety of seeds, berries, and animal matter.

About Flying Squirrels

These gliding mammals are much more common than most of us realize. Many a large wood with mature timber contains flying squirrels. Because they are nocturnal, silent, and remain hidden away by day, they are seldom seen, even by informed naturalists. Despite these habits, they are easily drawn into an appropriately placed feeding station that has sunflower seeds, peanuts, or other suitable food. Near the University of British Columbia, they visit a feeding station located on a seventh floor balcony. A bluebird-sized nest box placed reasonably high up (5-6 m / 16-20 ft.) in a coniferous tree may be used as a daytime retreat. Gnaw marks around the entrance often indicate "Flying Squirrel in residence" (Plate 10).

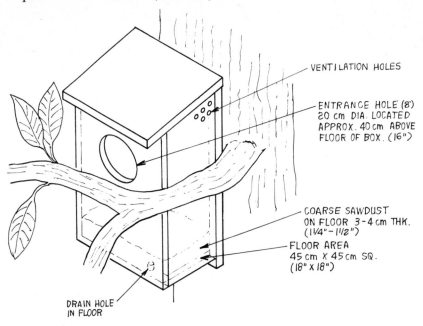

Figure 3.6
A raccoon roost box.

About Raccoons

Raccoons can be both a joy and a nuisance. They have adapted very well to our suburbs, and particularly to the way we handle our garbage. Though seldom seen by day, they are easily encouraged to visit nighttime feeding stations where they will accept a wide variety of foods. The raccoon's natural diet varies considerably with the season (Table 3.3).

In the presence of garbage or a well-stocked feeding table, these preferences and patterns disappear. Whatever is easiest becomes the raccoon's fare. At the feeding table, a raw, whole hen's egg is a particular treat.

Because raccoons have a propensity for "washing" their food, the presence of a nearby water source is an added advantage.

Raccoons, like other nocturnal animals, require a quiet, safe daytime hideaway. This can be an attic, a culvert, vacant building, or other suitable retreat. In natural settings, these sites are often large, hollow trees, hollow logs, a dense tangle of vegetation, or an old crow's nest. Providing a daytime den for raccoons (Figure 3.6) is not without risk of incurring property damage or the potential of a transmittable disease. However, if such a den is provided well away from a residence, the chances of risk are greatly reduced.

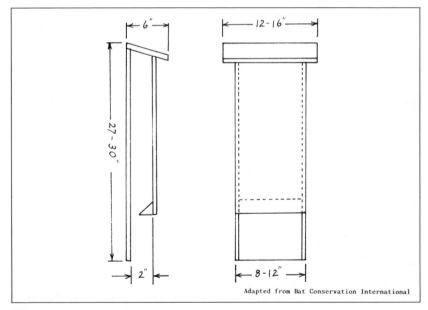

Adapted from Bat Conservation International

Figure 3.7
A 'generic' bat house.

Raccoons have a number of negative qualities that should concern the wildlife gardener. One is that they are serious predators of small animals and delight in raiding bird nests. When raccoons are around, protect bird nesting locations.

Like skunks, raccoons are subject to diseases such as rabies and distemper. Both canine and feline distemper affect raccoons and together these often regulate the raccoon population. For this reason, any skunk or raccoon that appears disoriented or is encountered under unnatural situations must be suspect. Never handle these animals.

TABLE 3.3
NATURAL DIET OF RACCOONS BY SEASON

Season	Plant / Animal	Specific Items
Spring	predominantly animal matter	large pond animals— crayfish, clams, water beetles, etc.
		young animals, birds, and eggs
Summer	about 70% vegetarian	berries, fruits, seeds, etc.
		vegetables, particularly corn
		pond life, minnows, frogs, etc.
Fall	predominantly vegetarian	nuts, fruits, and corn
		bee, termite, and ant larvae
Winter	mostly animal matter animal carcasses	stored body fat

About Bats

Though there are many species of bats, it is the small brown bats of the *Myotis* group that are most frequently seen around our homes and gardens.

As insect eaters, bats approach swallows in the number and volume of flying insects they consume. In rural conditions bats roost under bark, in hollow trees, and in caves. In urban set

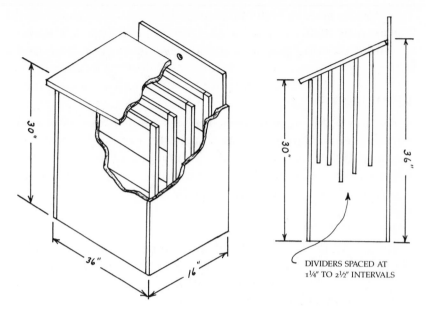

Figure 3.8
A larger bat house, with dividers spaced from 3.5 to 5.5 cm apart to accommodate bats of different sizes.

tings they use attics and other similar dark, quiet places with an appropriate entrance.

Bats have also been induced to use artificial "bat houses" (Figures 3.7 & 3.8). Depending on size, bat boxes can house a single individual or an entire colony. These structures have long been popular in Britain and are now being used in North America.

By providing this type of structure at least you will have a good idea where the bats around your house are roosting. In constructing the inside dividers use rough sawn timber to provide a good gripping surface for the occupants.

Bats may be encouraged to forage in a backyard by mounting a low-power light 4-5 m (13-16 ft.) above the ground (Figure 3.5), which is lit during the evening hours. Such a light has at least two benefits. As well as attracting flying insects which the bats may chase, the light also provides a degree of visibility for other nocturnal animals, such as flying squirrels and toads.

To some, bats have a bad reputation as they occasionally carry rabies. For this reason bats found in unusual places or circumstances should be handled with care.

Bats may also carry a number of other diseases. Therefore, potential roosting places in private dwellings should be closed off.

REPTILES

As opposed to salamanders, reptiles enjoy a warm sunny dry environment. Gardens with southerly exposures and open areas with lots of cavities and hiding places are ideal reptile habitats. Garter snakes, as well as turtles, enjoy sunning areas near ponds well stocked with aquatic life.

About Garter Snakes

Too many people consider snakes to be among the most loathsome of creatures. This is a sad commentary on our view of a very interesting and beneficial group of animals. Our garter snakes, for instance, should not be maligned as they are one of the major predators on slugs. For this reason the backyard gardener should consider the garter snake to be a prized ally rather than a despised invader.

Garter snakes generally prefer locations having a warm, sunny exposure with ample places to retreat and hide. Pacific Northwest species enjoy partially aquatic environments. In backyard settings, edges, garden banks, fish ponds, ditches, and semi-wild areas are favored garter snake habitats.

Garter snakes are surprisingly efficient underwater predators of small fish, salamander larvae, and tadpoles. They will frequently adopt a pool and remain "in residence" until the local food supply is diminished.

During the winter months our garter snakes hibernate in subterranean dens known as hibernacula. Such dens can be built into rock walls, rockeries, and hillsides by allowing adequate space between the rocks used as building materials. The depth should approach 1 m (39 in.) with consideration being given to preventing ground water from flooding the cavity.

About Painted Turtles

The Painted Turtle gets its name from the beautiful markings on its belly. In our area it is a common species that leads a highly aquatic life style. It readily adapts to a backyard pond well stocked with pond life and pond plants. Here they feed on snails, aquatic insects, tadpoles, small fish, and, as they get older, pond plants.

Painted turtles will "go walkabout", so a small fence will be required to keep them home.

Ponds for turtles should be at least 1.5 m (5 ft.) deep and have enough soft mud and decaying plant material on the bottom to permit hibernation over winter. Sunning areas, such as floating or partially submerged logs, and a short stretch of shoreline with loose, sandy soils for possible nesting meet their requirements.

Protection from raccoons is essential for small individuals.

About Lizards

The Western Fence Lizard and the Northern Alligator Lizard are the two most common species in the Pacific Northwest. Both will frequent open sunny locations in a garden with adequate space and cover.

The fence lizard, often known as a "swift" or "blue belly" is frequently seen on fence posts, rock and woodpiles, even on buildings. It is found from about Seattle southward. The alligator lizard occurs north into British Columbia where it enjoys semi-open areas with fissured rock, logs, loose bark, and similar hiding places. Both species feed on insects, spiders, and other invertebrates.

Occasionally the smooth, shiny, striped skink may wander into urban areas. The young of this species are noted for their bright blue tails.

Predators, especially cats, appear to be the limiting factor that prevents lizards from maintaining viable populations in suburban areas.

AMPHIBIANS

More than anything else, amphibians require moisture. Most species lay their eggs in water and all species require a moist skin through which they breathe. In a garden setting a well vegetated pool with nearby piles of moist organic debris make an ideal environment for these animals. To maintain the organic debris I 'high grade' my annual wood order, selecting the poor quality or rotting pieces for salamander use.

About Frogs

A number of species of frogs are found in our area with the most familiar being the tree frogs. These small (4 cm / 1.6 in.) bright green, grey, or brown frogs are noted for their noisy spring chorus from March through May. It is the tadpole of these species that many children bring home to watch transform from pollywog to tiny frog.

Once the breeding season is over these frogs move away from their birth ponds, where their agility and 'sticky' toes enable them to leap and climb through nearby vegetation.

Tree frogs will quickly accept a backyard fish pond with well developed emergent vegetation such as Cat-tail or Iris, species easily transplanted from the wild. Once established in a pond, tree frogs can be difficult to evict.

In coastal areas the Red-legged Frog, and in the interior and central areas, the Wood Frog and Spotted Frog, are three larger native species (6-7 cm / 2.4-2.8 in.) which frequent wooded streams and cool clean ponds. These species tend to be more solitary than the tree frog.

In the dry areas, spade-foot toads may breed in small, backyard pools. Their resonant croaking will delight the ear of the amphibian lover.

The Bullfrog is now a common species along the West Coast introduced from the east. This huge frog, with large conspicuous eardrums, frequents permanent water sources with dense growths of emergent vegetation. The giant tadpoles (to 15 cm/6 in.) of this species are quite a novelty and are occasionally sold in the pet trade.

If this frog is desired in a backyard setting, a fairly large pond will be required. Because Bullfrogs often prey on smaller amphibians, such as Tree frogs, their presence in a pool can be to the detriment of these species.

In spring the deep, resonant jug-o-rum or br-rum call of the bullfrog is distinctive.

Whatever the frog species, all require clean, cool, permanent water to complete their life cycle.

Plate 11
A backyard pool used by Salamanders.

About Salamanders and Newts

Smooth-skinned salamanders and granular-skinned newts are surprisingly common in undisturbed damp forest and aquatic habitats. Some species, such as the Red-backed Salamander, are totally terrestrial, while the Long-toed Salamander and the rough-skinned newts return to ponds each spring to breed.

The largest and perhaps the most striking of our salamanders is the Tiger Salamander, which is found from eastern Washington to the Great Lakes. They live near water under natural debris or in burrows of other animals. This is a large species. Adults and the larvae often become more than 30 cm (1 ft.) long. For the backyard pool they are best imported as larvae. The tiger Salamander is a voracious animal, consuming earthworms, large insects, other amphibians, even small mice.

In ponds, the larvae of salamanders are readily separated from frog tadpoles by their elongated shape and large bushy gills located just behind the head.

With urbanization, salamanders are among the first amphibians to disappear. Where properties adjoin undeveloped parks, or wild tracts of land, the provision of a breeding pond with submergent vegetation and clean water is beneficial to these species. Nearby, the maintenance of a moist shaded habitat, including piles of old or rotting wood, bark, stumps, and rocks, is desirable (Plate 11). During dry periods a liberal sprinkling with a garden hose will help maintain a moist environment.

CONCLUSION

The small mammals, reptiles, and amphibians have a special appeal to many people. Catering to the needs of frogs, lizards, turtles, and bats is a challenge that will require well vegetated pools, sunning areas, and night viewing facilities. Speaking as someone who has made this effort, I know you will find the rewards to be more than satisfactory.

4

Spring Gardens for Birds

Without question, songbirds are the most popular and desirable of all backyard wildlife. To ensure and encourage their presence, we annually spend millions of dollars catering to their needs. Because birds are so hyperactive, their main desire and their near-constant activity is their quest for food. However, beyond just supplying food, there are countless ways to ensure that these colorful, active, and by no means quiet songsters provide us year-round enjoyment.

As the seasons change, the general attractiveness of our gardens to urban birds also changes. As this happens, the backyard manager must modify his strategies and change tactics. The axiom for attracting birds is simply to supply what is most desired when it is most required. With some exceptions, these are nesting sites in spring, water in summer, and food and shelter in winter.

Because there is so much interest in birds, and so much information available, in this book each season is afforded its own chapter.

SPRING: THE SEASON OF RENEWAL AND ARRIVAL

Spring is the season when our common backyard summer birds begin their parade of appearance. In the interior, the procession begins as early as February with the appearance of the Common Crow and Red-winged Blackbird. These are followed

Plate 12
Swallow "Feed Me!" A young Violet-green Swallow in a simple nest box.

a short while later by the true harbingers of spring—the Violet-green and Tree Swallows. The parade culminates in late May with the overhead arrival and passage of the Common Nighthawk.

With the departure of winter snows and the greening of the countryside, supplemental feeding from bird feeders assumes lesser importance. Since natural foods are more readily available, you may wish to phase out your feeding station, even though a few resident birds may still be regular guests.

For birders, as birdwatchers are known, spring is an exciting season. Depending on weather patterns and cloud cover, many unusual species might arrive in your garden. A good bird book, particularly one of the popular field guides, and a pair of binoculars, are musts if you wish to know who's who. Simply watching and recording the species passing by during this season is a meaningful challenge.

As the migration subsides, the breeding season commences. For your backyard residents the ritual and preparation for this event becomes a preoccupation. Likewise, the backyard gardener should also focus his or her activities towards this event.

Bird houses are just one way of ensuring some species will nest on your property. Providing appropriate vegetation for those species which do not nest in bird boxes is a second consideration. A third is providing appropriate nesting materials.

Last and certainly not least, especially for your enjoyment, is catering to the likes of hummingbirds.

In addition to these activities the backyard gardener must think ahead to the summer, autumn, and winter seasons. In part at least, seed and fruit producing plants sown or planted in spring will reap benefits to be enjoyed later in the year.

BIRD HOUSES FOR THE NEST BOX NESTERS

Nesting structures are easily built from almost any type of materials, including ceramics, metal, and even plastics. Wood is the most readily available material, and is preferred because of its natural properties.

Nesting structures may be built in all manner of shapes and sizes. Those illustrated in Figure 4.1 and 4.2 are quite simple to make and in my experience have produced good results. Over the years, a great deal of sophistication has evolved to tailor

TABLE 4.1
NEST BOX MEASUREMENTS FOR COMMON BACKYARD BIRDS

Species	Size of Hole	Floor Area	Distance Hole Above Floor	Roof to Floor Depth	Height Above Ground
Swallows: Violet-green, Tree	2.5×4 cm (1×1.6 in.)	13×13 cm (5.×5.2 in.)	10 cm (4 in.)	12 cm (4.8 in.)	3–5 m (10–17 ft.)
Chickadees: Black-capped, Chestnut-backed	3 cm (1.2 in.)	9×9 cm (3.6×3.6 in.)	15 cm (6 in.)	23 cm (9.2 in.)	2–5 m (6½–17 ft.)
Wrens: House Bewick's	3 cm (1.2 in.)	1×10 cm (4×4 in.)	10 cm (4 in.)	18 cm (7.2 in.)	2–3 m (6½–10 ft.)
Bluebird: Mountain Western Eastern	4 cm (1.6 in.)	13×13 cm (5.2×5.2 in.)	15 cm (6 in.)	25 cm (10 in.)	2–4 m (6½–13 ft.)

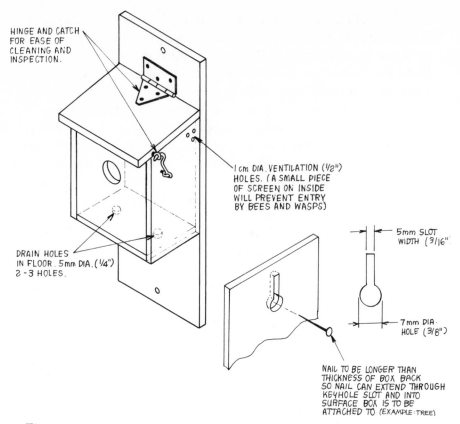

Figure 4.1
A simple practical nest box design with a 'key hole' device for mounting a nest box on a common nail.

these structures to the special needs of individual species. This is particularly true for bluebirds. The bluebird nest box illustrated in Figure 4.3 was designed for Western Bluebirds.

Robins and Barn Swallows require only a simple shelf or bracket. For the other nest box species, size, shape, and design are important considerations (Table 4.1).

Generally speaking, the simpler and more natural (in both shape and materials used) the better the chances of the nest box being used (see Plate xx). Paints and stains are not necessary. In fact, they may even be detrimental.

For a more detailed set of plans and a material list for the nest boxes illustrated, write to the author.

Once constructed, the next important consideration is choosing the right location.

SPECIAL FEATURES TO IMPROVE
NEST BOX PERFORMANCE

Having said that painting a box may be detrimental, it is interesting to note that nest boxes painted flat-black inside have a higher occupancy rate than unpainted boxes. When constructing nest boxes, use weathered natural or rustic materials whenever possible. Rough-cut red cedar, used previously in fences or as siding from old buildings, is an ideal material. If you have the patience and wish to age fresh cut cedar, leave it outside, exposed to the elements for at least a year! If you want to paint your nest boxes do this in the fall so that the paint vapors will be gone by spring.

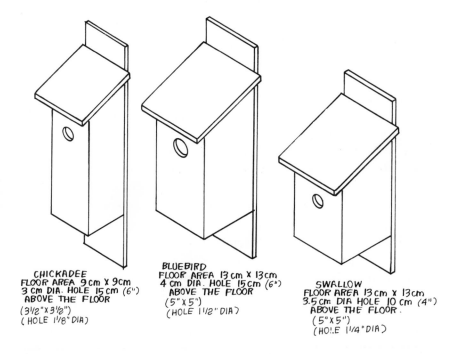

CHICKADEE
FLOOR AREA 9cm X 9cm
3 cm DIA. HOLE 15 cm (6")
ABOVE THE FLOOR
(3½"x3½")
(HOLE 1⅛" DIA)

BLUEBIRD
FLOOR AREA 13 cm X 13cm
4 cm DIA. HOLE 15cm (6")
ABOVE THE FLOOR
(5"x5")
(HOLE 1½" DIA)

SWALLOW
FLOOR AREA 13 cm X 13cm
3.5 cm DIA HOLE 10 cm (4")
ABOVE THE FLOOR.
(5"x5")
(HOLE 1¼"DIA)

Figure 4.2

Modifications to the simple nest box making it more attractive to chickadees, bluebirds, and swallows.

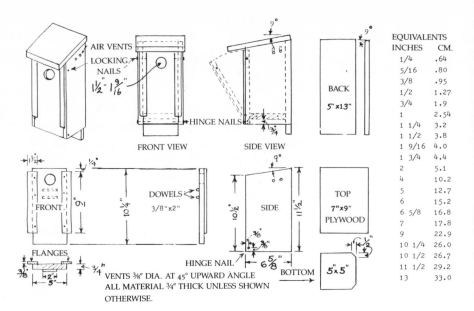

Figure 4.3
A sophisticated nest box specially designed for bluebirds.

NEST BOXES FOR HOUSE SPARROWS AND STARLINGS

To wildlife watchers, House Sparrows and European Starlings are controversial species. Despised they may be by some, but their presence can bring joy in areas where few native birds may be found. Both species build large, untidy nests. Nest boxes for them require fairly large entrances, 4 cm (1.6 in.) for House Sparrows and 5-6 cm (2.0-2.4 in.) for starlings. The other measurements should equal those given for bluebirds in the case of House sparrows, and larger than those given for bluebirds in the case of starlings.

Here are a number of suggestions to discourage these species from using nest boxes intended for other species.

1. Make the hole oval in shape (e.g. 4 cm / 1.6 in. wide and 2.5 cm / 1.0 in. high) or triangular in shape (3.6 cm / 1.4 in. each side), which is better suited to swallows (and frustrates House Sparrows) (Figure 4.4).

2. Keep boxes small and deep for chickadees or move the hole down to 3 cm (1.2 in) above the floor for swallows.

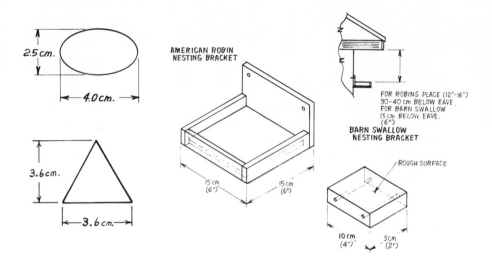

Figure 4.4
Hole sizes and shapes to deter
House Sparrows.

Figure 4.5
A Robin shelf and a Barn
Swallow nesting bracket.

3. Block the entrance with paper or hold off putting up boxes until late April or early May.

4. Place boxes in a location where you can easily scare away or harass unwanted nesters.

5. Locate boxes for wrens and chickadees in partially secluded locations screened by deciduous vegetation (wrens) and evergreen vegetation (chickadees).

6. For swallows, increase the thickness of the front panel to 3-3.5 cm (1.2-1.4 in.) to make the hole more like a tunnel.

NEST PLATFORMS FOR ROBINS AND BARN SWALLOWS

Both these species are partial to nesting under the eaves of houses where a suitable platform exists. For robins, a platform at least 15 x 15 cm (6 in. x 6 in.) with a slight lip placed 30 cm (12 in.) below the eave against the wall will give good results. For some reason greenery in the form of plastic foliage placed around the edge of the platform improves results.

For Barn Swallows, a 10 cm (4 in.) block of 2 x 3 board nailed or glued 15 cm (6 in.) below the eave will provide enough support for their mud nests (Figure 4.5). Rough wood is best as it improves the sticking power of the mud.

For information on species nesting in unwanted locations see Chapter 11.

THE 'DO IT THEMSELVES' SPECIES

Woodpeckers, chickadees, and nuthatches will build their own nest boxes if a suitable snag is present. These snags can either be created or imported. Creating a snag by girding a live tree and waiting takes a long time for the wood to reach the appropriate softness for these species to excavate easily. Hardwoods such as alder, maple, and birch are the best species to use because they deteriorate more quickly than softwoods. To hasten the softening process, suitable logs, 3-5 m (10-16.5 ft.) in length and 15-30 cm (6-12 in.) in diameter may be placed on moist ground and/or covered with leaf litter in the fall. One to two years of this treatment should soften the wood to the desired state.

FINDING THE RIGHT PLACE FOR A NEST BOX

1. Understand the preferences of the species for which the box was built. For example: swallows and bluebirds require a clear, open approach. Chickadees and wrens appreciate a little seclusion.
2. Avoid exposure to: full sun, prevailing winds, driving or heavy rains. Easterly or westerly exposures are considered best.
3. If a number of boxes are being put up, try to space them well apart, and/or have them face different directions. This lessens competition. In most instances the average backyard can only accommodate three to four boxes at the most—each usually designed for a different species.
4. Try to avoid areas where predators are present or areas which have easy access for predators such as cats and squirrels. Squirrel guards may be required.

ANNUAL MAINTENANCE

After the nesting season, old nests may be removed and the boxes given a thorough cleaning. A good hosing with soapy water or disinfectant to wash out all fine materials, including parasites, their larvae, and eggs, will make the box more hygienic for use next season.

The reason behind this annual maintenance program to remove potential parasites is not as simple as it might seem. Parasites have parasites too!

One of the common parasites, particularly of young Barn Swallows, is a species of blowfly whose maggots suck blood from nestling birds. Once these larvae pupate, they in turn may be parasitized by a variety of tiny wasps. This complex relationship of birds to blowflies to wasps (and no doubt the wasps have parasites too!) has evolved over eons.

When it comes to bird house maintenance, a rigorous cleaning with disinfectants disrupts this local balance. From the bird and birder's point of view this may be well and good. While there are many interesting and practical arguments on both sides of the question of intervening in such a natural chain, the important thing to remember is that we still have Barn Swallows, even though they nest naturally and are exposed to parasites.

Nest boxes are not natural cavities. Generally, when we compare natural cavity sizes to those recommended for bird houses, the natural ones are quite a bit smaller, more compact, and require less nesting material. Therefore, there might be less space for potential parasites.

From this, perhaps there are two lessons to be learned. First we should make our nest boxes a little smaller, and second, the simple removal of old nesting materials each spring should be the extent of our annual maintenance program.

TREE AND SHRUB NESTING SPECIES

Providing nest sites for the tree and shrub nesting species is not as easy as making the preparations for the nest box crowd. Often it takes a number of years for a tree or shrub to reach the desired size and form. Even when it has reached this stage it is still the bird's choice when it comes to choose which tree or shrub. Table 4.2 is a compilation of the nesting records from the British Columbia Nest Record scheme (Chapter 9) operated by the Royal British Columbia Museum.

TABLE 4.2
NESTING INFORMATION ABOUT SOME COMMON BACKYARD BIRDS IN B.C.*

Species	Location	Nest Height	Breeding Chronology	Preferred Vegetation
Rufous Hummingbird	Coastal	1–3 m (3–10 ft.)	—nest building, early April	—native evergreens Western Red Cedar
			—young may leave nest up to mid-July	Douglas Fir Sitka Spruce
				—vines: blackberry
	Interior	1–2.5 m (3–8 ft.)	—nest building, begins early May	—native evergreens Englemann Spruce
			—young may leave nest up to very early August	Western Red Cedar Douglas Fir Ponderosa Pine
				—orchard trees
Cedar Waxwing	Coastal	1.5–6 m (5–20 ft.)	—nest building begins late May	—native evergreens Douglas Fir
			—young may leave nest up until mid-August	—native broadleaves, Vine Maple, Broadleaf maple
				—ornamental trees English Hawthorn
	Interior	1.5–5 m (5–17 ft.)	—nest building begins late May	—orchard trees Apple Pear
			—young may leave nest up until late August	—ornamental trees Lilac Russian Olive
				—native evergreens Englemann Spruce Douglas Fir
				—native shrubs Wild Rose Mock Orange
House Finch	Coastal	1.5–5 m (5–17 ft.)	—nest building begins late March	—ornamental evergreens Cedar Juniper Spruce
			—young may leave nest up until mid August	—native evergreens Douglas Fir

House Finch (cont.)				—hanging flower baskets
				—Ivy walls
	Interior	1.5–3 m (5–10 ft.)	—nest building begins late March	—ornamental evergreens Cedar Juniper Spruce
				—native evergreens Douglas Fir Englemann Spruce
				—orchard trees Apple
Chipping Sparrow	Coastal	1–3 m (3–10 ft.)	—nest buildings beings early May	—native evergreens Douglas Fir
			—young may leave nest up until late July	—orchard trees Apple
				—Shrubs Scotch Broom
	Interior	3–3.5 (10–12 ft.)	—nest building begins in mid-May	—native evergreens Douglas Fir Engelmann Spruce Juniper
			—young may leave nest up until early August	—orchard trees Apple Pear
				—native shrubs Wild Rose Snowberry
Dark-eyed Junco	Coastal	On ground	—nest building begins early April	—nest located on dirt banks, rock walls, and occasionally in hanging baskets
			—young may leave nest up until late August	
	Interior	On ground	—nest building as above begins mid-April	as above
			—young may leave nest up until mid-August	

*Data taken from British Columbia Nest Record Scheme

With the exception of the Dark-eyed Junco, which is a ground nesting species, most of the common backyard birds show a distinct preference for fairly mature native evergreen and orchard trees, such as the apple. To some degree, all trees and shrubs can be improved as possible sites through careful pruning. This should aim to provide small clumps of thicker or denser foliage against trunks or along limbs.

In the average backyard, House Finches are perhaps the most regular garden nesters, showing a preference for ornamental evergreen shrubs. Nonetheless, a dash of luck is still present.

TABLE 4.3
SOME PREFERRED NESTING MATERIALS USED BY COMMON BACKYARD BIRDS

Materials	Species used by
straw—course	robin, starling, sparrow,
—fine	junco, finches
string (short lengths)	robin, chickadee, oriole
moss	chickadee
lichen	hummingbird
rootlets	siskins
twigs and cedar bark	crows
hair—horse, deer	Chipping Sparrow, chickadees
—domestic pets	
feathers	Barn, Violet-green and Tree Swallows
cotton, kapok, bulrush	wrens, chickadees, hummingbirds
mud	robins, Barn and Cliff Swallows

NESTING MATERIALS

At some time or another, just about every conceivable material might find its way into a bird's nest. While string, straw, feathers, and mud are the most common items used in nest construction, cellophane, shoelaces, and even snake skins are not unknown. Some common household and garden materials used by our native birds are listed in Table 4.3, although this list is not exhaustive.

If you have one of the swallow species nesting near your home you may wish to "feed" them feathers! About the middle of May, when nest building is nearing completion, Violet-green, Tree, and Barn Swallows actively search for feathers to line their nests. During this period it can be great fun to drop feathers from an elevated window or porch and watch the swal-

Plate 13
Rough and rustic, a bird house built from bark slabs and intended for Brown Creepers.

Plate 14
An onion bag filled with bullrush down. A good way to dispense nest lining materials.

lows catch them as they drift by on the breeze. Downy white feathers seem to be favored.

Nesting material for birds can be dispensed in a number of ways. An onion bag is an easy way to hang out these materials (Plate 14). Mud too, can be prepared and put out on a small sheet of plastic or a puddle can be kept moist with a regular sprinkling of water.

HUMMINGBIRDS

Many different types of birds are known to be nectar feeders, species which actively seek out flowering plants that produce copious quantities of sweet liquid. The list of species worldwide is quite diverse, but two families noted for this practice are the sunbirds of Africa and the honeyeaters of Australia. Neither, however, can match our hummingbirds for color or variety, or can compete with them as subjects of human interest. These gorgeous jewels of the bird world are a common element of the backyard scene. Our area is blessed with at least

Plate 15
An Anna's Hummingbird at a
winter feeder in southwestern
British Columbia.

Plate 16
House Finches at a
hummingbird feeder modified
for their easier use.

five species. In early spring at the time the Red-flowering Currant and Salmonberry break into blossom, the first of the migrant species, the Rufous Hummingbird, arrives along the west coast. Along inland valleys, the Rufous, Calliope, and Black-chinned species time their arrival with the blooming of other flower types. To the east, the Ruby-throated hummingbird is the species present. Very recently, the Anna's Hummingbird has become a year-round resident, wintering in areas as far north and inland as the Rocky Mountains. It is believed that hummingbird feeders are largely responsible for this situation.

The continued presence of hummingbirds around the garden can easily be encouraged by either planting nectar producing flowers and shrubs that bloom in succession (Table 4.4) or by providing sugar-water feeders. These latter devices are readily available in a variety of commercial models, or they can be made from easily procured materials (Figure 4.6).

TABLE 4.4
FLOWERS ATTRACTIVE TO HUMMINGBIRDS

Native Species	*Horticultural Species*
SHRUBS:	TREES:
Red-flowering Currant	Horsechestnut
Ribes sanquineum	*Aesculus* species
Lobb's Gooseberry	Locust
Ribes lobbii	*Robinia* species and varieties
Salmonberry	Catalpa
Rubus spectablilis	*Catalpa* species
Pentstemon	
Pentstemon species	SHRUBS:
	Butterfly Bush
VINES:	*Buddleia davidii*
Orange Honeysuckle	Lilac
Lonicera ciliosa	*Syringa* species and varieties
	Siberian Pea
FLOWERS:	*Caragana arborescens*
Columbine	Weigela
Aquilegia species	*Weigela* species and varieties
Bee Balm	Flowering Quince
Monarda species and varieties	*Chaenomeles* species and
Scarlet Gilia	varieties
Impomopsis aggregata	
Cooley's Hedge-nettle	VINES:
Stachys cooleyae	*Scarlet Runner Bean*
Tiger Lily	
Lilium columbianum	Trumpet Creeper
Fireweed	*Campsis radicans*
Epilobium angustifolium	
Foxglove	Nasturtium
Digitalis species	*Tropaelolum majus*
Phlox	
Phlox species and varieties	FLOWERS:
Alyssum	Fuchsia
Alyssum species	*Fuchsia* species and varieties
	Petunia
	Petunia species
	Touch-me-not
	Impatiens species
	Gladiolus
	Gladiolus species
	Delphinium
	Delphinium species and
	varieties
	Sage
	Salvia species

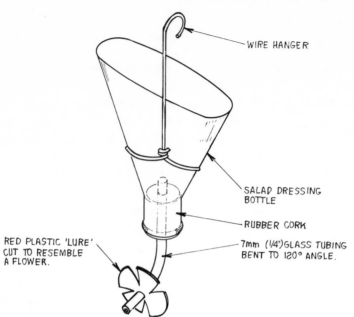

WIRE HANGER

SALAD DRESSING
BOTTLE

RUBBER CORK

RED PLASTIC 'LURE'
CUT TO RESEMBLE
A FLOWER.

7mm (1/4")GLASS TUBING
BENT TO 120° ANGLE.

Figure 4.6
A simple 'do it yourself' hummingbird feeder.

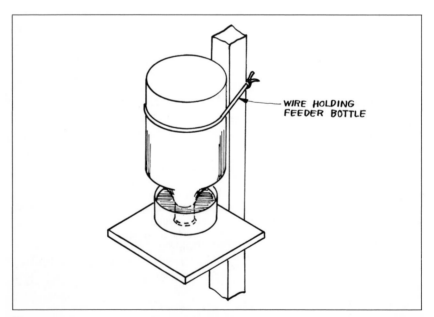

WIRE HOLDING
FEEDER BOTTLE

Figure 4.7
A House Finch sugar-water dispenser.

Sugar Water Recipes for Use in Hummingbird Feeders

Much has been written about the strength of the sugar solution that should be provided for hummingbirds. Most recommend a solution of one part by volume of white granulated sugar to two, three, or four parts of water. One study by a student in Victoria, British Columbia, showed that when given a choice Anna's Hummingbirds preferred a sugar solution of 75 percent (75 g sugar in 100 ml water) over all others.

Most hummingbird flowers are known to produce nectar with low sugar concentrations. On this information a solution of one part sugar to three or four parts water is recommended.

A Note About Additives

Red food coloring: While red is a well-known attraction to hummingbirds, the addition of red food coloring to the sugar water solution does little to improve the end result. As long as the feeder has a red "lure" when it is first placed outside each season, the hummingbirds will quickly learn how to find the solution. Once this happens the lure almost becomes unnecessary.

Honey: Honey in its commercial forms is dangerous to hummingbirds as it may cause fungal growths in their throats. Apparently the only safe honey is honey straight from the hive. **As few of us have easy access to an apiarist, perhaps the best thing to do is not to use honey at all.**

Fermentation: Natural yeasts and molds are everywhere and it is quite possible they will begin the fermentation process inside your feeder. This happens more quickly during hot weather or in the presence of other additives to the basic sugar water.

To reduce the chances of the sugar water solution from spoiling, wash your feeder thoroughly between each filling. When the weather is hot replace the unused solution every second day. Again, wash the feeder between fillings. By using boiling water in your recipe, most spores will be killed. Once the solution has been allowed to cool, it is then ready for use. Surplus solution can be stored in your refrigerator.

Hummingbird Dependence and Addiction

Hummingbirds quickly become dependent on feeders and the number of individuals present can be excessive. Often there are not enough suitable flowering plants nearby to sustain the population should you want to stop feeding, or take a summer vacation. Once a feeding station is started it must be continued, or phased out gradually. This may mean asking a neighbor to fill it for you during your absence.

Control of Wasps, Bees, and Ants

These insect may be attracted to your hummingbird feeder. For measures to control them, see Chapter 11.

House Finches at Hummingbird Feeders

House finches have also shown a preference for sugar water feeders. Depending on your preferences, House Finches can be encouraged by adding perches (see Plate 16), or discouraged by removing perches from your feeder. When House Finches are really numerous, sugar water can be dispensed from a water bottle (Figure 4.7).

A Natural Association

White birch, the Red-naped Sapsucker, and our hummingbird species may seem like an unusual combination, but they do have an affinity for one another. Birch trees produce a high quality sap, favored and worked by the sapsucker. Around these workings hummingbirds, bees, and some other insects rob and steal the sap when the developer is absent. Around developed sap wells the feeding activity of these species can be phenomenal.

While the backyard gardener cannot be guaranteed that his or her birch tree will become a sapsucker tree, having a White or Paper birch as part of the garden shrubbery opens the door should a sapsucker take up residence in the neighborhood.

SPRINGTIME PLANTINGS FOR
SUMMER, FALL, AND WINTER

Suggested plantings of flowering and seed producing plants with values for wildlife appear throughout this book. The backyard wildlife gardener must be selective and, in consultation with the local nurseryperson, choose those species which best suit local environmental conditions.

Spring is the best time for sowing the seeds for many of these annual species (Table 4.5).

Transplanting of perennial species and some biennials as well, can often be done in either early spring or fall. Again, your local nurseryperson is the best source of information. Collecting the seed of annual species has to be done during the previous flowering season. Storage in a manner to ensure sprouting is often tricky. Once these plants are established they should become self sustaining from one season to the next.

In pond or marsh areas the Smartweeds *Polygonum* species) and Pondweeds (*Potamogeton* species) are good seed producers for aquatic birds.

TABLE 4.5
SOME SEED PRODUCING PLANTS ATTRACTIVE TO BIRDS

NATIVE GRASSES	
Panicgrass	*Panicum* species
Crabgrass	*Digitaria* species
Bristlegrass	*Setaria* species
FLOWERING PLANTS	
Knotweeds	*Polygonum* species
Pigweeds	*Amarantinus* species
Lambs Quarter and Goosefoot	*Chenopodium* species
Miner's Lettuce	*Montia* species
Chickweeds	*Cerastium* species
Cranesbill	*Erodium cicutarium*
Ragweeds	*Ambrosia* species
Dandelions	*Taraxacum* species
Sunflowers	*Helianthus annuus* (also horticultural/agricultural varieties)
Thistles	*Cirsium* species—particularly *C. vulgare*
Cosmos	*Cosmos bipinnatus* and varieties

5

Summer Gardens for Birds

As spring warms into summer, the heralding of each new day brings with it the crescendo of bird song—the dawn chorus. Following nest building and egg-laying, this chorus slowly subsides into the uneasy quiet of late July and August. Then, almost without notice, the first of our summer residents begin to slip quietly southward. Soon, they are only a memory. Table 5.1 lists some common backyard summer birds.

Songbirds time their breeding cycle to coincide with the most favorable weather and abundant food resources. However, because summer is the dry season, water becomes a limiting factor. The need for water can be easily satisfied in backyard gardens. A carefully planned water source or a variety of water sources can become a real attraction to summer birds.

A second and somewhat lesser need is a quiet, secluded, and protected place where young birds can pass through their adolescence and learn the skills needed for survival.

While summer is noteworthy for its abundance of natural foods, the backyard gardener should be aware that the berry season begins with the appearance of ripe Salmonberries during early June. These are favored by robins and thrushes. Other plant species with fruits attractive to birds are listed in Table 5.2.

TABLE 5.1
COMMON SUMMER BACKYARD BIRDS

	West Coast	Interior	Eastern
California Quail	*	*	
Rufous Hummingbird	*	*	
Ruby-throated Hummingbird			*
Violet-green Swallow	*	*	*
Barn Swallow	*	*	*
Black-capped Chickadee	*	*	*
Bewick's Wren	*		
House Wren	*	*	*
American Robin	*	*	*
Yellow Warbler		*	*
Yellow-rumped Warbler	*	*	*
Northern Oriole		*	
House Finch	*	*	*
American Goldfinch			*
Chipping Sparrow		*	
White-crowned Sparrow	*	*	
Song Sparrow	*	*	*

TABLE 5.2
SOME SUMMER FRUITING TREES AND SHRUBS ATTRACTIVE TO BIRDS
WITH APPROXIMATE FRUITING TIMES

Species	June	July	August	September
Bitter Cherry *Prunus emarginata*			————	————
Cascara *Rhamnus purshinanus*				————
Western Flowering Dogwood *Cornus nuttalli*				————
Salmonberry *Rubus spectabilis*	————			
Thimbleberry *Rubus parviflorus*		————		
Himalayan blackberry *Rubus discolor*			————	————
Red Huckleberry *Vaccinium parvifolium*		————	————	
Hawthorn *Crataegus species*				————

SINGING STATIONS

As well as visual enjoyment, birds also provide joyful stimulation to our sense of hearing. Almost without exception, all our backyard birds, even the hummingbird, have their particular sounds, calls, or songs. During courtship display and territory formation in particular, our backyard birds sing their hearts out. Identifying the species present simply by their songs can be an interesting challenge. Once mastered, you can just about throw away your bird books and binoculars and conduct a roll call of the species present using only your ears!

During these solos each individual songster will have its favorite perches or singing station. Often these are in the open; but sometimes they are screened. In shrubs and small trees, perches can easily be developed by simply girdling the bark on an upright stem or lateral branch. Not only will this produce a bare twig as a perch, but it will also stimulate new growth which will improve shelter for possible nest sites.

WATER

Next to food, nothing is more attractive to birds than a good, safe, shallow supply of clean water. While water is an every-season need, summer is the season when birds need water most of all. Most birds drink it, many bathe in it, and a few even dunk their food in it.

ABOUT BIRD BATHS

These water sources should be kept shallow with gently sloping sides if they are to be used for bathing. A non-skid surface is a second prerequisite. Avoid plastic, metal, fiberglass, or other slick surfaces. Slightly roughened concrete is ideal.

Your local garden shop or nursery will have a variety of sizes, shapes, and styles of bird baths available. Check them carefully for cracks and flaws. Baths with flat rims and gently sloping sides are best. Water depth in the center should be about 6-8 cm (2.4-3.2 in.).

If you have the time, energy, and a creative flair, you can easily build an attractive bathing area at a chosen location with a small amount of cement.

Plate 17
Commercial water sources
available from farm supply
companies. These provide a
source of drinking water only.

Plate 18
Bird baths of commercial
types placed in appropriate
locations.

Locating Your Bird Bath

Like bird nest boxes and bird feeders, the location of a bird bath is very important, especially for small birds. Perhaps because bathing is a very active indulgence that quickly draws attention, placing a bird bath near shrubbery is important. Around my own backyard pool, a shallow embayment has been covered by a loose canopy of branches (Plate 4). Here, chickadees, siskins, and crossbills bathe regularly. Before the canopy was created, this area was used infrequently.

Should Band-tailed Pigeons find your pool, do not be alarmed by the white powder that remains floating on the surface after their bathing sessions. This dandruff-like powder may be part of their feather maintenance system. Should one of these pigeons strike a window an imprint from this powder will remain.

To improve use of a birdbath you may wish to elevate it into the branches of a larger tree. This will keep it away from predators such as cats. This can be accomplished by placing the bath in a sling and using a pulley to raise it to the desired height and location. If a dripping hose can be located above the bath, use should improve considerably.

ADDING NOISE

If water is an attraction, dripping water can be a magnet, especially to small birds on hot days. Drippers, as these noise makers are often called, may be created in a number of ways. A slightly loosened faucet, with or without an attached hose, placed above the shallow portion of the bath can produce enough noise to attract birds from a considerable distance. A bucket with a small pin hole in the bottom placed above the pool can produce a similar result (Figure 5.1).

Figure 5.1
Two simple ways of creating a dripper for a bird bath.

AIR CONDITIONERS

The by-product of air conditioning is water distilled from air being passed through the conditioning unit. Why waste this precious commodity? Trap it if you can, and by means of a hose or tube, direct it to a location where it can provide relief for birds, insects, and other animals which frequent your yard.

ANOTHER WATER SOURCE—
YOUR LAWN SPRINKLER

Watering lawns to keep them green, fresh, and soft is an important means of keeping robins, Chipping Sparrows, and other species in your yard. These watered places become important feeding areas when nearby areas become hard and dry.

Hoses and sprinklers directed as a fine spray into shrubs and the lower branches of trees often prompt small birds to take a shower. By flitting through the spray and bumping into the saturated foliage, they drench their feathers, achieving the same effect as taking a bath. In some instances, Bushtits become so wet they cannot fly until their feathers dry out.

CARE AND MAINTENANCE OF WATER SOURCES

Clean, clear water sources quickly become tainted and contaminated under heavy use. Unmanaged bird baths may also harbor and transmit diseases. During periods of hot weather and heavy use, a regular hosing and occasional scrubbing are important in maintaining the bath's attractiveness. This treatment may be required on a daily basis.

ONE LAST WORD ABOUT SUMMER WATER—
CROWS, THE FOOD DUNKERS

In addition to bathing, crows love to dunk their food in water before eating it. A water source for this purpose should be somewhat deeper than a bath, though bird baths are often used. It is also desirable to place this water source away from areas frequented by smaller birds.

DUST BATHS

Water is not the only substance used by birds for bathing. Grouse, quail, and House Sparrows are particularly partial to dusting. In dry sheltered locations, with loose fine soils, a scrape can be developed in which the birds flop and flutter to move the tiny dust particles through their feathers. Just like water, the dust acts as a cleansing agent and also discourages external parasites.

The sheltered sunny side of a building or boulder, a protected bank or the base of a tree are all ideal dusting sites. Once established, dust baths will be used from season to season and from year to year.

FEEDING SUMMER BIRDS

Oranges for Orioles

The Northern Oriole is not found in all regions, but where it occurs its vivid orange, black, and white plumage makes it unmistakable. For its color alone it is a welcome, if not highly prized, visitor to any garden. Orioles are largely frugivorous, which means fruit eating. Attract them into your garden by providing sectioned oranges placed or wedged into the forks of branches as high up as you can conveniently place them.

Goldfish for Kingfishers

While it might seem inhumane, you can attract predators to your garden by supplying them their appropriate foods. While few bird feeding people would acknowledge it, their feeding stations attract bait for Sharp-shinned and Cooper's hawks, and occasionally small owls.

These are not the only predators you could attract to your garden. Many people who have backyard pools grimace for good reason at the mention of Great Blue Heron and Belted Kingfisher. These birds steal their goldfish! Should you have a backyard pool, you could stock it with local fish, or visit your local pet shop and bulk-purchase goldfish sold as feeder fish for the aquarium trade. Such a purchase could be considered a modest price to pay for the stately presence of a heron or the rattle of a kingfisher some quiet morning. One thing I can tell you from personal experience is that the white goldfish disappear first, the orange next, and the black ones go last—an interesting lesson in the survival of the fittest through natural selection.

6

Autumn Gardens for Birds

As the days shorten and the nights grow cooler, excitement grips the air as our native birds bunch up in anticipation of their pending southward migration. Restlessness and a degree of nervousness pervade the flocks which gather around abundant food resources.

A few years ago the bickering of a hundred voices in some nearby yew trees sparked a curiosity which led to a memorable outdoor experience. In the trees overhead, birds of nearly a dozen species were feasting, gorging themselves on the red, ripe berries of the female yew trees. Patience and careful observation revealed a much more fascinating story. Yes, it was a banquet of sorts, and yes, many of the birds were feeding, but each species was feeding in quite a different manner.

Robins and thrushes simply plucked and ate the pulp and seeds together. Western Tanagers ate only the fruit, pulp, carefully leaving the skin and seed to drop to the forest floor. Chickadees plucked the seeds from the fleshy aril and then proceeded to split out the kernel. Evening Grosbeaks also ate only the seed after shearing away the flesh and cracking the seeds in their massive bills. The remaining species—sapsuckers, juncos, siskins, and nuthatches—may have been attracted by the noise and commotion. I never observed them to feed on the fruit.

Piecing together this puzzle provided an inner satisfaction and the strong indication that each species' feeding methods were quite different.

Not every garden will have a female yew tree loaded with fruit, but careful observation can provide you with some fascinating insights into the behavior and "personalities" that separate one species of backyard bird from another.

With the appearance of small flocks of the northern migrants, we know summer has truly faded into autumn. As the season chills into winter, supplemental food sources assume greater importance to those individuals and species which intend to remain.   Autumn is the time to winterize your garden and prepare for winter needs.

Work Required
1. Ready or build your winter bird feeders.
2. Add additional cover to brush piles and protection around feeders.
3. Gather preferred native foods, e.g., Mountain Ash berries.
4. Improve shelter, cover, and wind break effectiveness of hedges and shelter belts.

EXPECTING THE UNEXPECTED

Our small songbirds usually migrate southward at night when sky and weather conditions are favorable. Should unusual weather conditions such as winds, clouds, or fog develop, these flights are terminated and the would-be migrants drop back to earth, sometimes well off course. During these freak times many unusual species can suddenly appear. In autumn, however, the bright crisp plumages of spring have often changed dramatically. Autumn might be called the season of the small, dull, brown birds, that seem impossible to identify. Have patience, and practice. Do not despair—even the experts have trouble. Nonetheless, keep a sharp eye out. Some very unusual species turn up in each year.

Spring and fall are the two seasons to expect the unexpected!

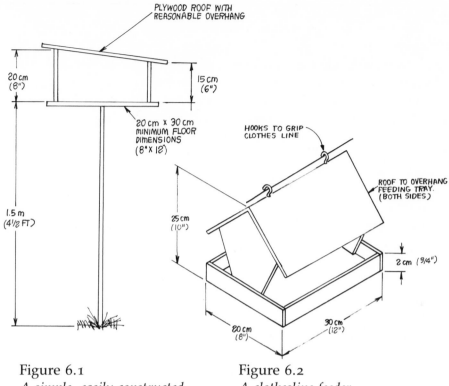

Figure 6.1
*A simple, easily-constructed
bird feeder.*

Figure 6.2
A clothesline feeder.

BIRD FEEDERS

Bird feeders, like bird houses, can be built in many shapes
and sizes. The one overriding consideration for all feeders that
dispense seed is that of keeping the seed as dry as possible.
Wet seed will often mildew and spoil. The types of feeders illustrated in Figures 6.1 - 6.5 have been used successfully for
many years. For a detailed set of these plans and a material list,
write the author.

Suet feeders can be a simple wire basket (Figure 6.5) or a
coarsely woven bag (such as an onion sack) in which the suet is
placed. The bag is then suspended using a length of wire in a
suitable location. For the wire hook, a coat hanger is ideal. During mild weather, pieces of suet can quickly spoil and become
rancid.

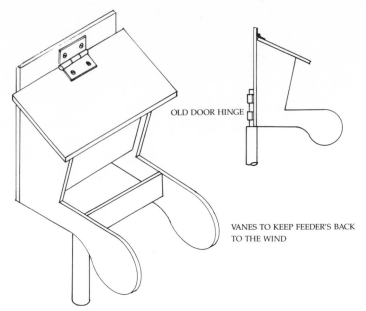

Figure 6.3
A weather-vane feeder, designed to keep food dry.

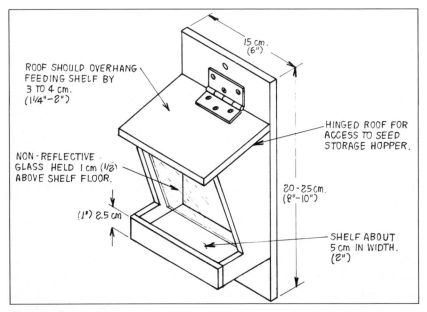

Figure 6.4
Rough plans for a hopper feeder.

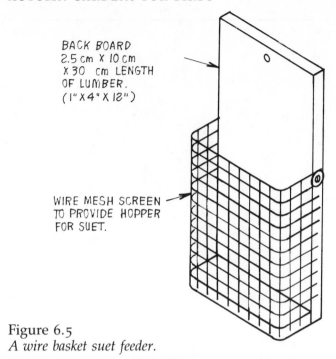

BACK BOARD
2.5 cm X 10 cm
X 30 cm LENGTH
OF LUMBER.
(1" X 4" X 12")

WIRE MESH SCREEN
TO PROVIDE HOPPER
FOR SUET.

Figure 6.5
A wire basket suet feeder.

Plate 19
A sample of commercially available bird feeders.

Plate 20A
*Building a teepee brush pile
—good protection for small
birds when built near a feeder.*

Plate 20B
*To provide more protection
hang evergreen branches over
this framework.*

BUILDING A GOOD BRUSH PILE

Brush piles are simply piles of brush, branches, and other woody material. Building a brush pile with maximum value for winter birds and other wildlife requires special care. The end purpose should be to create an internal space or chamber with perches for the occupants that are a fair distance above the ground. Two meters (6-7 ft.) would be a good height for a wild-life brush pile.

One way to accomplish this is to select eight or ten sturdy, straight but untrimmed branches and arrange them in a tepee-like circle with their butt ends planted firmly a short distance into the ground. Allow or make their finer ends interlock skyward. On top of this, pile evergreen branches or other suitable materials to form the dome. Each year add a few new branches to the top and sides (Plate 20).

If the brush pile is started in the spring, climbing plants such as scarlet-runner beans, honeysuckle, virginia creeper, clematis, morning glory, pumpkins, or squash can be planted to grow over the pile. This will provide an attractive and practical decoration.

In the fall, corn stalks also make a good addition to the pile. Brush piles with part of one side left slightly open can become a good feeding area for small, ground frequenting birds.

THE BRAMBLE PATCH

The stoutly armed Himalayan and Evergreen blackberries (*Rubus procerus* and *Rubus laciniatus*) provide impenetrable tangles of dense vegetation that offer ideal cover for songbirds and other wildlife. Even Peter Rabbit of Thornton Burgess fame took refuge in his briar patch. In addition to cover, the ripe fruit from these vines is actively sought by a number of birds, not to mention humans who find blackberry pie and blackberry jam quite delectable.

Despite these benefits, the disadvantage of having a blackberry patch in the average garden lies in keeping these invasive, thorny shrubs in check. Since new shoots may grow 5 m (16.5 ft.) or more in a season, and their root systems are difficult to eradicate, few gardeners may wish to live with these plants. Should a patch of blackberries occur nearby, perhaps they should be tolerated, even though considerable effort may be required to keep them under control.

7

Winter Gardens for Birds

Few activities bring people more enjoyment than feeding birds during our dull winter months. Despite our intemperate climate the number and variety of species which remain is quite diverse. Christmas bird-counts for coastal areas of British Columbia record about 130 species annually; for the interior valleys 90 species; for the far eastern valleys about 50 species. Of these, the number that may frequent a backyard feeding station is quite diverse (Table 7.1).

Even though winter is the time when only the hardiest bird species remain, their needs are quite modest and relatively easy to satisfy. A well located and appropriately stocked feeding station will become a great attraction. Careful attention to providing different foods in different but appropriate locations will separate the larger birds from the smaller, as well as attract a broader range of species.

In addition to food, the presence of cover to provide shelter from prevailing winds, for refuge, and for roosting, is also important. A third need is fresh clean water.

With these elements in place, line-ups at your feeder will be the order of the day as species and individuals await their turn. At these times your enjoyment will be endless.

TABLE 7.1
SOME REASONABLY COMMON BACKYARD WINTER BIRDS

Species	West Coast	Interior	Eastern
California Quail	*	*	
Anna's Hummingbird	*		
Northern Flicker	*	*	*
Downy Woodpecker	*	*	*
Hairy Woodpecker	*	*	*
Steller's Jay	*	*	
Blue Jay		*	*
Black-capped Chickadee	*	*	*
Chestnut-backed Chickadee	*		
Red-breasted Nuthatch	*	*	*
White-breasted Nuthatch		*	*
Bewick's Wren	*		
American Robin	*	*	*
Varied Thrush	*		
Bohemian Waxwing		*	*
Evening Grosbeak	*	*	*
Purple Finch	*	*	*
House Finch	*	*	*
Pine Grosbeak		*	
Pine Siskin	*	*	*
American Goldfinch	*	*	*
Rufous-sided Towhee	*		
Dark-eyed Junco	*	*	*
White-crowned Sparrow	*		
Golden-crowned Sparrow	*		
White-throated Sparrow			*
Fox Sparrow	*		
Song Sparrow	*	*	*

WINTER BIRD FOOD PREFERENCES

It seems clear from studies conducted in eastern North America that there are striking differences in the attractiveness of the different seeds we present to our winter birds (Table 7.2). When purchasing packaged bird seed mixes, it is desirable to know the preferences for those species which frequent your feeding table. Putting this knowledge into practice will help you to increase the numbers and variety of birds, as well as save money by avoiding waste.

The studies done in the east found unattractive foods to be buckwheat, whole wheat, peanut hearts, hulled oats, and rice. Personal experience in the Vancouver area indicates peanut hearts are a very popular winter bird food.

TABLE 7.2
COMMERCIAL SEED PREFERENCES OF SOME WINTER BIRDS*

Seed Type	Species
White Proso Millet	House Sparrow
	Song Sparrow
German Millet	House Sparrow
Red Proso Millet	Dark-eyed Junco
	Song Sparrow
Sunflower Seeds	Chickadees
	House and Purple Finch
	Evening Grosbeak
	Red-breasted Nuthatch
Canary Seed	Dark-eyed Junco
Peanuts	Steller's Jay
	Blue Jay
Wheat	none
Hulled Oats	European Starling
Cracked Corn	Dark-eyed Junco
Thistle	American Goldfinch

*from published sources

During the winter of 1987-88, I tested five commonly available, wild-bird mix ingredients on a small mixed flock of songbirds in Nanaimo. Table 7.3 shows the results.

On the subject of feed preferences, two points should be remembered. First, in special circumstances or under adverse conditions, almost any type of food, even those not normally attractive, may be consumed in great quantities. The second is that by knowing likes and dislikes, you may find that inexpensive foods give the best results. Therefore, at your feeding station, do not be afraid to experiment or vary the menu! And keep notes on the results and your observations.

OPERATING A WINTER FEEDING STATION—
SOME GENERAL CONSIDERATIONS

There is therapeutic value in having an active birdfeeder. You can sit and watch it for hours as the parade of individuals and species succeed one another—an avian soap opera, complete with villains and saints. From this perspective, birds around a window feeder, like fish in your dentist's aquarium, offer relaxation not to be underestimated.

TABLE 7.3
FEEDING PREFERENCES OF WINTER BIRDS—NANAIMO,
BRITISH COLUMBIA

Commercial seeds	Dark-eyed Junco	Rufous-sided Towhee	Chestnut-backed Chickadee	House Finch	Song Sparrow	Fox Sparrow
Small black (Oil-type) sunflower seeds	33%	70%	89%	95%	5%	79%
Peanut Hearts	29%	14%	11%	5%	61%	14%
White Proso Millet	17%	1%				15%
Chick Scratch	13%	10%			19%	
Wheat	8%	5%				7%
	100%	100%	100%	100%	100%	100%

A feeding station is a supplementary food source at which our winter birds will spend varying amounts of time. Some individuals, who become addicted, will always be present. Those either less addicted or who prefer to forage for naturally occurring foods will only be transients. Whatever the case, once a feeding program is well underway it should continue until natural foods are again readily accessible. In times of severe weather, a well-stocked and protected feeding station may be essential to a small bird's survival through difficult periods.

To be effective, a feeding station does not have to cater to every species likely to be found in your area. One feeder supplied with sunflower seeds and a second with a mix of millet or other small grains should reap the greatest rewards. If, along with these, a couple of suet bags are hung out, you will be catering to the majority of species found around your home.

KEEPING FOOD DRY

Keeping food dry, particularly seed grains, is very important. Wet grains quickly develop molds which increases the risk of disease. For this reason, do not hesitate to sweep or clean out your feeder on a regular basis, especially those with flat feeding surfaces.

Three measures to keep your seed offerings as dry as possible are using feeders with a good overhang to the roof; placing your feeder in a sheltered location protected from prevailing winds or driving rains; or using a fine screen as the feeder platform. This latter method, which may require support rods to prevent the screen from sagging, allows moist seed to dry quickly.

A FEW NOTES ABOUT SOME COMMON COMMERCIAL BIRD FOODS

About Chick Scratch: This commonly available product is a mixture of cracked corn and cracked wheat. Among the small seed eating birds such as sparrows and juncos, it is fairly popular. However, in the presence of other small whole seeds, such as millet or canary seed, it is often passed over.

About Sunflower Seeds: There are a number of different types of sunflower seeds sold on the market. These are described in a number of different ways. They may be black or striped, small or large feeding, roasting, or oil type. All types appear to be popular to backyard birds. Feeding your birds sunflower seeds can be an expensive proposition, particularly if a large flock of Evening Grosbeaks discovers your feeding station. Since the smaller black sunflower seeds are cheaper, with more seeds per measure, these appear to be the most economical type to use. They appear to be the most preferred by birds.

About Peanut Butter: Fresh peanut butter can cause birds problems due to its stickiness. Its texture is changed somewhat when the peanut butter is placed outside in a cold environment where it hardens. To reduce its stickiness, mix in any one of a number of ingredients including rolled oats, corn meal, chick scratch, or other similar grains that will absorb some of the oil. In this hardened state, birds are better able to peck off small pieces and swallow them without harm.

About Suet: While true suet is the best animal fat to feed wild birds due to its granular nature, it is seldom available from your butcher. In fact, it usually has been removed at the packing house. The next best thing is 'cod fat.' Ask your butcher for

TABLE 7.4
OTHER FOODS EATEN BY WINTER BIRDS

Food Item:	
Suet	Woodpeckers
	Chickadees
	Jays
	Nuthatches
Chick Scratch	Dark-eyed Junco
	Song Sparrow
	White-crowned Sparrow
	Golden-crowned Sparrow
Chopped Peanuts or Peanut Hearts	Chickadees
	House Finch
Peanut Butter Mixes (see text)	Woodpeckers
	Jays
	Chickadees
	Nuthatches
Fruit—apples	Robins
—Mountain Ash berries	Bohemian Waxwing
—crabapples	Varied Thrush
hawthorn berries	
Pyracantha and Cotoneaster berries	Robin
	Varied Thrush
	Townsend's Solitaire

this by name, and if there is none available he will probably provide you with a suitable substitute at no cost. In this day of prepackaging, large modern supermarkets no longer cut their own meat. Therefore, you may have to seek out a butcher who sells beef in sides and quarters.

About Bread and Kitchen Scraps: Leftovers from our tables are often provided as food to wild birds, but they are not readily accepted by the smaller species. More often they are readily accepted by House Sparrows, starlings, jays, gulls, and crows—species generally considered to be less desirable. Feeding scraps on a regular basis encourages these larger birds, and while they may provide a lot of entertainment, they often bully away the smaller, perhaps more desirable species.

Feeding birds dry bread during severe weather is better than feeding them nothing at all, but, compared to the commercially available seed grains, bread has much less food value.

TABLE 7.5
SOME FRUIT-PRODUCING TREES AND SHRUBS ATTRACTIVE TO BIRDS
IN AUTUMN AND WINTER

Native	Horticultural
Columbia Hawthorn *Crataegus columbiana*	English Hawthorn *Crataegus laevigata*
Black Hawthorn *Crataegus douglasii*	Mountain Ash *Sorbus aucuparia*
Pacific Crabapple *Pyrus fusca*	Crabapple *Malus—many species*
Arbutus *Arbutus menziesii*	Holly *Ilex aquifolium*
Garry Oak *Quercus garryana*	Firethorn *Pyracantha coccinea* and varieties
Choke Cherry *Prunus virginiana*	Cotoneaster many species and varieties
Broad Leaf Maple *Acer macrophyllum*	Honeysuckle *Lonicera* species
Douglas Maple *Acer glabrum*	
Vine Maple *Acer circinatum*	
Paper Birch *Betula papyrifera*	
Orange Honeysuckle *Lonicera ciliosa*	
Dogwood *Cornus* species	

About Alcoholic Apples: This may sound strange, but every winter somewhere in our area, robins, Varied Thrushes, Bohemian Waxwings, and European Starlings imbibe the fermented juices of frozen, unharvested apples. The choruses and high jinx from these tipsy birds verges on the ridiculous, with casualties the result. There is little you can do (other than remove all the fruit), except to watch the party and then assist those individuals who get into trouble. Put them in a 'drunk tank'—a warm, dark, secure box—and when they are over the effects, slowly acclimatize them to the outside environment before releasing them.

GRIT

Many small seed-eating birds, and some of the larger birds as well, rely on grit to help them pulverize or grind the food in their crops. When heavy snow blankets the ground, their natural sources of grit are removed. Providing some sand with variable sized grains up to 3 mm (1/8 in.) diameter on the floor of your feeder will supply this need. **Do not** add grit to your bird food recipes. Not all birds require grit. Besides, I'm sure you wouldn't appreciate pebbles in your lasagna!

PROVIDING WATER IN WINTER

Birds appreciate water, even during the coldest periods of the year, for drinking and bathing. In winter, keeping this water supply from freezing is a problem. Two ways to solve this dilemma include the use of an electric light bulb or an electric heat tape. To keep the heat tape stationary, wrap it around a piece of pipe (Figure 7.1). Thermostatically controlled heating units, suitable for use in a bird bath, are now available commercial to provide water during even the coldest periods.

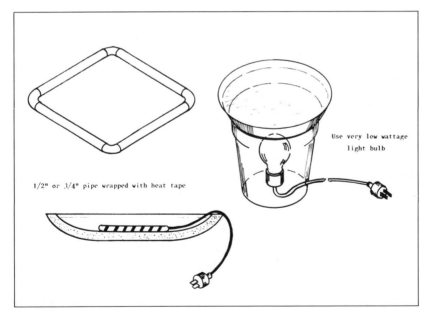

1/2" or 3/4" pipe wrapped with heat tape

Use very low wattage light bulb

Figure 7.1
Two ways of providing water for birds during cold weather.

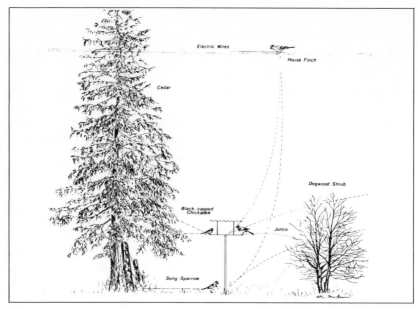

Figure 7.2
Approach route and feeding locations of some common winter birds at a backyard feeder.

If your water supply is being used constantly, check it frequently to make sure the water remains clean.

WINTER BIRDS NOT ATTRACTED TO FEEDERS

While many winter species find bird feeders hard to resist, there are a few species which seldom make an appearance. From my experience, these include Pine Siskin, Common Redpoll, and the Golden-crowned Kinglet. Surely, among the varieties of food and recipes available, there is one delicacy that might tempt these species. Who knows what this is?

LOCATING YOUR FEEDER

Around your feeding station each species has its preferred routes of approach (Figure 7.2), its preferred feeding location, and a preferred feeding method. For instance, juncos and Song Sparrows sit and pick while chickadees grab and run. Keeping these preferences in mind, a few other considerations for locating a feeder include visibility of the feeder from your window, shelter from prevailing winds and weather, and the availability of nearby cover for escape from predators. In choosing an appropriate location, these factors need to be balanced in the best possible manner.

Placing feeders in the open where we can see them easily leaves the users vulnerable to hawk attacks. Feeders for small birds should be placed as near to cover as possible. Better still, surround them partially with protective vegetation. Having a few branches that extend beyond the feeder not only provides convenient perches but also foil predators.

WINTER BIRD FOOD RECIPES

Nearly every person who regularly feeds birds in his or her backyard has favorite recipes for the feathered visitors. Generally speaking, these recipes are a mixture of two ingredients: fat, usually as suet or peanut butter, and seed grains of a wide variety. Fruits, kitchen scraps, and bread are a few other ingredients used frequently.

For exotic seeds, such as niger (thistle), buckwheat, and poppy seed, contact a pet shop or garden shop that caters to cage bird enthusiasts.

While working on the manuscript for this book, a hyperactive flock of Bushtits provided an enjoyable diversion. They buzzed around a mixture of drippings, peanut butter, and rolled oats. This stiff paste had been pushed into holes on a 5 cm (2 in.) diameter tree trunk, where numerous side branches on the tree provided perches for the whole flock.

The recipes included here are but two of many that have appeared over the years.

Please remember that fats become soft or rancid during warm weather. Putting these out only during the cooler months may prevent birds from soiling their feathers as they feed. Avoid bacon grease—the salt content is very high.

Nuthatch and Chickadee Balls

Cut up or grind one pound of suet. Heat slightly until suet softens and becomes sticky. Stir in enough whole or shelled sunflower seeds (about 1 cup / 250 ml) so that the mixture becomes stiff.

Plate 21
A simple yet effective elevated feeder for small birds. This type of feeder can also be hung on a clothesline.

Figure 7.3
The 'Butling' cone feeder.

Roll into 5 cm (2 in.) diameter balls and cool in refrigerator or freezer. Hang outside in mesh bag as needed.

The Crawford Bird Food Recipe

Prepare a sugar syrup by adding one cup of sugar to three cups of water. Bring this to a boil and add one pound (500 g) of suet (available at your supermarket). Add 1/2 cup (125 ml) of peanut butter and one cup of either cream of wheat or oatmeal cereal. Allow mixture to cool. If still too liquid, add a little more cereal.

When thickened: roll mixture into balls and place in an onion string bag or wire screen container; or, force between scales of a large pine cone (Figure 7.3) and hang upside-down with a piece of wire (squirrels chew through string!); or, pour mixture into a 48-oz. (1.3 L) juice tin and push cone into mixture, wait till it thickens slightly, then extract cone. This mixture is an excellent winter diet.

8

Planning Your Wildlife Sanctuary

Planning is the carefully thought-out, orderly provision of shelter, food, and water, to maximize a garden's attractiveness to urban wildlife. The planning process comprises five distinct functions: site selection, site analysis, drawing up a rough or conceptual plan, making a final plan, and building your garden. Planning concludes when you have created your garden and evaluated your results. In previous chapters we looked at the needs of wildlife, identified some of the common species likely to be present, and also provided a number of ideas you may wish to incorporate into your garden. The planning stage begins when you bring all your likes, dislikes, and ideas together and start to formulate the plan for your garden.

The first step in this process is site selection. Unless you are in the process of purchasing a home or property, this part of the process will be a given. For those purchasing a home or property, the questions posed in Chapter 1 under the heading of Taking Stock should prove helpful.

In this chapter we will be concerned largely with the remaining planning stages. This is where you consider the questions what, where, and how. At this stage it might be wise to start putting your ideas down on paper. Having gone through this exercise a number of times, I find it to be a very helpful practice—even when the final result differs from what was first envisaged.

SITE ANALYSIS

This stage involves the inventory and evaluation of the features already present on site. As you walk around your property, record the size of the following:
• other buildings such as garages and storage sheds
• decks, patios, pools, sidewalks, and paths
• existing trees, shrubs, flowers, and vegetable gardens
• stumps, rock piles, embankments, and ditches
• natural water sources—including downpipes
• good views from windows to be kept unobstructed and poor views to be screened
• location of fences and borders

Some Other Features of Importance
• water and sewer lines, drains, and underground tanks
• powerlines and telephone cables
• prevailing wind directions

One Axiom Worth Remembering
"It takes diversity to reap variety."

This might better be explained as follows. The greater and more varied the features you can incorporate in your garden, and the greater the variety of plant species present, the greater should be the variety of wildlife species you can expect to attract.

A FEW OTHER CONSIDERATIONS

Edges: The interface or edge between open space and dense vegetation is the area favored by most wildlife. It is also the place where wildlife is the easiest to observe. While the average city lot will not have enough area to create long edges, by planting the tallest and densest trees—usually evergreens—around the perimeter of your yard and shrubs towards the inside, you can create an interesting edge zone. To develop such an edge from scratch may take many years. In planning and developing these edges, consider diversity in both height and breadth of your plantings, and try to maximize both.

Zoning: Because all species of wildlife are not compatible, you may wish to consider zoning your garden in such a manner to enable you to cater to preferred species at one location. You can zone your garden in a number of ways besides simply providing for different species in different locations. For instance, you can take advantage of a species' behavior, abilities, or food preferences, or you can alter the time when certain needs are provided for.

Examples:

Using Behavior - At feeding stations juncos and Song Sparrows are generally ground feeders. House Finches, which enjoy some of the same foods, prefer feeding from elevated feeders (Figure 4.2).

Using Abilities - Squirrels cannot climb pipe posts to feeders intended for birds. Starlings cannot enter nest boxes with holes less than 3 cm (1.2 in.) diameter, but swallows can.

Using Food Type Preferences - Starlings do not normally pick up small seeds whereas juncos and Song Sparrows will.

Using Time - Food put out at dusk will remain for Flying Squirrels and Raccoons and will not be taken by grosbeaks and crows.

AVENUES OF VIEW

One of the major considerations of the wildlife garden is to be able to see the birds and other creatures from your windows. Therefore, in the conceptual planning stage make sure you provide and take advantage of good sight lines into the corners of your garden.

THE ROUGH PLAN

With your ideas clearly thought out and the above considerations in mind, now is the time to formulate your rough plan. You can quickly pencil it onto a scrap of paper or blackboard. Some people like to use cut-outs of the various ideas and plantings to shuffle them around their property space to create an imaginary garden. This allows you to try out different configurations. If each object is to scale, it will be a great help when it comes to drawing up the final plan.

THE FINAL PLAN

When you have all your ideas sorted out, draw up your final plan on graph paper. Try to keep your ideas to scale. Keeping things to scale is important. This will give you a much better perspective of how your ideas fit in relation to one another. Figure 8.1 is a stylized plan indicating a general arrangement for a typical backyard. This plan incorporates many of the ideas outlined earlier. One additional piece of information you may wish to include is contour or elevation lines. This is especially true if someone else is going to do the initial contouring.

To complete this plan, all that remains for you to do is to include names of the trees, shrubs, and flowers you wish to plant. These names can be taken from the lists in this book.

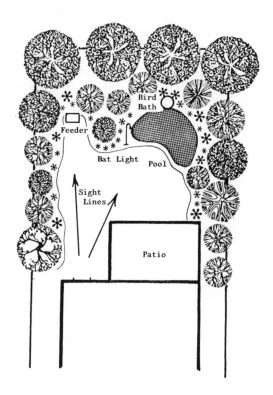

Figure 8.1

A stylized plan for an average backyard. Tall trees to the outside, shrubs to the inside.

Armed with the detailed plan, it will be much easier to explain your wants to others, not to mention the saving of time during actual construction.

Once your contouring and planting are complete, you will have your baseline garden. You may wish to enhance it by providing artificial sources of food, water, and shelter. These include pools, baths, feeders, lights, and nesting or shelter structures.

EVALUATION

Just because your garden is constructed it is not finished. At this point you cannot simply sit back and rest on your laurels. Now is the time for constructive criticism and formal evaluation of your masterpiece. From your own observations you may wish to modify your creation, to fine-tune it in order to make it even better. This is a challenge to last a life time!

See Chapter 9, Observing and Keeping Records, for helpful information on this aspect of evaluation.

Just Like Rome—Your Garden Will Not Be Built in a Day

The old cliche that Rome was not built in a day applies equally to your wildlife garden. However, by putting time on your side and exercising patience—time can work for you. In my formative years my father would tell me "little and often". Now, through hindsight, the wisdom of his words rings true.

For heavier tasks, bite off manageable pieces of work one at a time. In my great wall, I tried to fit at least ten rocks in place each weekend. In half a year the task was virtually complete. At one a day, 365 can be done in a year. Persistence and patience will reduce the greatest task. If you need a little variety, work on two or three jobs concurrently!

Gardening for Wildlife

Gardening practices to improve a backyard setting for wild-life are many and varied. Basically they relate to improving the habitat's ability to provide food, water, and shelter.

Good wildlife gardens need not be, and are best not, precisely laid out, neatly manicured areas. Some order and planning is desirable, as we have seen in Chapter 8. Perhaps an appropriate description of a good wildlife garden would be one with an untidy order, verging on planned chaos!

Some years ago, naturalist Yorke Edwards wrote a delightful piece about an apple tree in his garden. In edited form it is presented here because it provides an uncommon appreciation of backyard gardening.

The oldest, ugliest tree in my garden is the best in my opinion, for it is an apple that every year produces the miracles that someone has named Gravenstein apples.

Give me a Gravenstein, picked warm and perfumed in the autumn sun, and you can have all the leathery skinned Mackintoshes and every tasteless Delicious Apple in the world.

My Gravenstein also gives me an endless crop of pleasure because it is no sterile apple factory. It is a community teeming with life. To me such a variety of life is a more precious and valuable thing than apples, even Gravenstein apples.

When parts of the tree die, the bark loosens and, especially in damp warm weather, the wood lice hide here from the sun. An apple man once told me to get rid of all the loose bark because he said "bugs" hide under it. I didn't tell him that I leave it there for the same reason.

When I pruned off the dead limbs, I left some stubs hoping for Downy Woodpeckers. And downys came, made a nursery there, and raised a family. Then for six years running, that apple tree yielded a crop of Chestnut-backed Chickadees. In the process it also yielded six years of pleasure from my watching.

In summer, the Violet-green Swallows swoop low over my tree; in the autumn it is the hunting ground for swarms of Common Bushtits; in winter the House Finches sun themselves there on warm days and in February a Bewick's Wren begins to proclaim the spring from a high perch.

On top of this, my Gravenstein gives me blossoms, and shade, and apples.

To recognize that a thing can be good—and worth saving— simply because it is good to look upon, or to hear, or to smell, or to touch, or to think about goes far beyond gains in dollars, amounts of wood, or pounds of apples.

Because many features such as sidewalks, fences, patios, pools, and hedges can be precise to the point of being geometric, many other features such as composts, brush piles, weed patches, snags, and many of the more attractive plants can counterbalance this regimentation. While the result may appear untidy, this does not mean that the garden is unmanaged or that it is being purposefully neglected. After all, weeds and natural litter are favored haunts of many fascinating creatures.

Common sense, along with an understanding of the basic needs of backyard wildlife, should be the guiding principles for gardeners when providing for backyard animals. Providing for these needs in a backyard garden need not be elaborate, onerous or overly time-consuming.

WEEDS

While the gardening enthusiast may dislike weeds with a vengeance, it should be remembered that in reality a weed is really a "flower growing in the wrong location". Though most weeds do not have the color or foliage of their cultivated counterparts, their value to wildlife should not be underestimated. In the backyard garden, having a really good weed patch is an asset and not a liability. Selectively encouraging good weeds with wildlife value in a corner of a garden will provide not only natural foods but also natural cover.

Some good wildlife weeds are listed in Table 9.1.

TABLE 9.1
SOME GOOD WILDLIFE WEEDS

Species	Life Cycle	Comments
Thistles *Cirsium* species *Carduus* species	biennial (perennial)	favored by butterflies and goldfinches
Milkweed *Asclepias* species	perennial	a butterfly favorite
Lamb's Quarters *Chenopodium* species	annual	seeds favored by song birds (House Finch)
Knotweeds & Smartweeds *Polygonum* species	annual	seeds favored by song birds and upland game birds
Chickweed *Stelaria media* *Cerastium arvense*	annual	seeds favored by song birds
Dandelion *Traxacum* species	perennial	favored by goldfinches and Pine Siskins

DEVELOPING A WEED PATCH

Despite notions to the contrary, weeds do not grow just anywhere. Good wildlife weeds require an open, sunny location with moist, not soggy, soils of average texture. Once these requirements have been met at your desired location, there are two methods, other than pure chance, by which the appropriate weeds can become established. You may either collect the seed from plants nearby and scatter or shallowly bury these in the fall, or you may transplant their seedlings (if you can identify them!) to the chosen location early in the spring.

For biennial species, a degree of patience is required as it takes thistles and mullein, for instance, two years until they flower. For these species, odd and even year generations will be required if you desire their presence on a year-to-year basis. Note: The creeping Canada Thistle (*Cirsium arvense*) and some other weeds with underground runners can become a serious nuisance, difficult to eradicate. If you wish to plant these, do so in a tub or other container.

FRUITS AND VEGETABLES ATTRACTIVE TO WILDLIFE

Real conflicts develop over who deserves the fruits from a backyard garden. Do they belong to man or beast? The contest is usually a split decision, though man often seems to come off second best. While all cultivated fruits and vegetables are not equally attractive to wildlife, there are a few standouts (Table 9.2).

TABLE 9.2
FRUITS AND VEGETABLES WITH WILDLIFE VALUES

Species	Comments
Apple	Winter food—robins, waxwings, starlings, etc. Nesting—robins, House Finches
Cherry	Food—robins, tanagers, House Finches, starling
Corn	Food—raccoons, game birds, etc. Stacked stalks—teepee style—provide shelter.
Sunflower	winter food—chickadees, grosbeaks, and many other species
Grape *Vitis* species	When trained to grow against a wall or over a trellis, good nesting cover for birds is provided. Riverbank Grape (*V. riparia*) as an escape from cultivation, is known for its vigorous growth.

TABLE 9.3
QUICK COVER SPECIES

Species	Comments
Trees	
Willows *Salix* species	Suckers and shoots often root easily when pushed into soft, moist soil.
Poplar Particularly Lombardy Poplar *Populus nigra italica*	As above. Note: Roots are invasive. Do not plant near sewer or drainage lines etc.
Horticultural Shrubs	
Butterfly Bush *Buddleia davidii*	Grows like a weed—many varieties available. Easily started from cuttings. Pruning improves form and lengthens blooming period.
Weigela	Grows quickly—becomes ragged unless pruned—many color varieties available.
Fast Growing Perennial Vines	
Clematis species	Good, colorful vines for fences and trellises.
Virginia Creeper *Parthenocissus quinquefolia*	Deciduous leaves turn bright red in fall—attractive to birds.
Boston Ivy *Parthenocissus tricuspidata*	Semi-evergreen—makes fast, dense wall cover.
Hops *Humulus lupulus*	Grows quickly, needs rich soil, lots of water, and a sunny location. Attractive to insects which become bird food.
English Ivy *Hedera helix*	Evergreen, woody vines. Large dense tangles used by raccoons as daytime retreats.
Morning glory *Ipomoea* species and *Convolvulus arvense*	Provide colorful tangles
Sweet Pea *Lathyrus odoratus*	Colorful aromatic flowers. Good for screens.
Broad-leaved Peavine *Lathurus latifolius*	Perennial vine with white to magenta flowers.
Edible Pea many varieties—tall ones best	Use as dual-function, cover and food; seed favored by towhees and game birds.
Gourds—many varieties Pumpkin—many varieties Squash—many varieties	May be trained to grow over trellises, brush piles, etc.

QUICK SOLUTIONS FOR BARREN AREAS

Waiting for attractive or beneficial trees and shrubs to grow to an appropriate size and form may take the better part of a lifetime. Quick solutions are available to fill in gaps or spaces. While these may not be the ideal, they will permit a degree of acceleration that will buy time until the more desirable and preferred species attain the form and prominence desired. As soon as the desired species reach sufficient size the stand-ins can be pruned back, relocated, or eliminated. Some fast-growing species for barren areas are listed in Table 9.3.

Annual vines such as peas, beans, and squash can be allowed to grow over brush, piles, and stumps. At season's end, these can be left in place to provide additional cover and improve shelter during winter months. Replant the following spring if desired.

Perennial vines, such as Clematis, Honeysuckle, Morning Glory, or hops can be trained to grow along fences, trellises, and walls. Those species having the ability to attach themselves to walls, fences, and large tree trunks, such as Ivy and Virginia Creeper, will not require other support.

Quick screens can also be developed by burying the butts of branches in the ground to form a hedge and then training the climbers to grow up and between these supports. Some species of willow, cottonwood, and poplar will readily sprout and root by simply sticking a branch or sucker in the ground.

A list of hardy trees and shrubs with wildlife value are listed in Table 9.4.

INSECTICIDES AND HERBICIDES

Every gardener, at one time or another, infuriated by weed or insect pests, feels the urge to do something about them. Often the easiest solution is to spray them with chemicals, probably one of the commonly used herbicides or insecticides. Even when applied in the most careful and diligent manner, under ideal conditions, their effect often goes far beyond our intent. In most cases we have no idea what the result of our application has really been.

Insecticides are bad for wildlife, not only because they kill insects for which they were intended, but also because many of

TABLE 9.4
SOME TREES AND SHRUBS FOR INTERIOR AND NORTHERN
LOCATIONS

Green Ash *Fraxinus pennsylvanica*	Thrives on moist soils, tolerates severe cold but foliage burns in hot, dry weather.
Black Cherry *Prunus serotina*	Grows in a variety of soils, producing fruit every 3 to 4 years.
Crabapple *Malus* species	Many varieties available, small fruited species like Siberian Crabapple (*Malus baccata*) most often used by birds.
Silver Maple *Acer saccharinum*	Fast growing but weak. Tolerates a variety of soils.
Box Elder (Manitoba Maple) *Acer negundo*	Grows in a variety of conditions. Seeds and suckers readily.
Russian Olive *Eleagnus angustifolia*	Fruits ripen in summer and persist through winter.
Autumn Olive *Eleagnus umbellata*	Similar to above but more sprawling and shrub-like in form.
Nanking Cherry *Prunus tomentosa*	A tough, hardy shrub that produces small scarlet fruits.
Tatarian (Siberian) Dogwood *Cornus alba*	Hardy red branching shrub that produces small white berries.
Amur Maple *Acer ginnala*	Hardy shrub or small tree, foliage turns scarlet in fall.

the chemicals used remain in the environment and the food chain. Here they persist, building up, sometimes to lethal levels in organisms higher in the food chain.

Herbicides, though directed toward plants, are often poisonous to animals as well.

Two insecticides which appear fairly safe to vertebrate animals are Pyrethran™ and Rotenone™. Neither of these accumulates in the environment nor enters the food chain. While manufacturers may insist that 2-4-D™ and other herbicides are completely harmless if applied correctly, common sense dictates that they should not be applied to your garden. In many cases there may be some practical, safe alternatives to the use of these chemicals. Always consult with a person knowledgeable and qualified in the application of these agents.

ROBINS AND LAWNMOWING

Though it is known that robins are more successful in locating prey in longer grass, they have a distinct preference to forage in short grass areas such as lawns. Mowing will often induce a short term increase in the number of robins feeding on your lawn!

HEDGEROWS

Hedgerows, particularly in more open country such as farmland, are very important to wildlife. In the average backyard a hedgerow may not be required, but it could be effective. Table 9.5 lists some common coastal and interior plant species that make good hedgerows.

These thorny tangles, when interspersed with one or two evergreens, perhaps Douglas Fir or Lodgepole Pine, provide excellent cover and much natural food. Some useful additions include Multiflora Rose (*Rosa multiflora*) and, in the interior, Russian Olive (*Eleagnus angustifolia*). These species have high wildlife values.

TABLE 9.5
COMMON TREES AND SHRUBS OF HEDGEROWS

Coastal	Interior
English Hawthorn *Crataegus monogyna*	Douglas Hawthorn *Crataegus douglasii*
Pacific Crabapple *Malus fusca*	Blue Elderberry *Sambus cerulea*
Nootka Rose *Rosa nutkana*	Wood's Rose-Nootka Rose *Rosa woodsii, Rosa nutkana*
Snowberry *Symphoricapus albus*	Snowberry *Symphoricarpus albus*
Willow *Salix* species	White Clematis *Clematis liqusticifolia*
Himalayan blackberry *Rubus discolor*	

LITTER AND COMPOSTING

Litter, in the form of leaves, bark, and small branches, accumulates in any wild area as part of the transformation from vegetation back into soil. It is a very important part of the ecosystem, especially critical to many types of wildlife including wolf spiders, earthworms, salamanders, and towhees. For gardeners, the other side of the coin is the messy appearance of litter. As the litter decomposes to become a more homogeneous part of soil, it provides a multitude of environments characterized by being loose, moist, and organic.

Depending on the tree species overhead which supply the majority of the litter, different habitats are created. Those under coniferous trees in constant shade will have plant and moss species not likely to be found under deciduous trees. Likewise, the animals present will be different as well.

The question faced by the gardener is, "Do I allow this litter to accumulate or do I constantly clean it up?" If you are fortunate enough to have a large yard, perhaps you might delineate an area with a log or curb beyond which you allow natural litter to accumulate.

To enhance your "litter zone", particularly for salamanders, a few old logs or scattered chunks of decaying wood are helpful. A light hosing during dry weather, to maintain the moisture level, is also beneficial.

CONSTRUCTION OF ROCK WALLS
AND EMBANKMENTS

Old fashioned rock walls, laboriously constructed from field stone, provide wildlife with lots of shelter in the form of crevices and cavities. Today, barbed wire and mesh fences have largely replaced stone walls where artificial divisions of property are desired. However, a well-constructed rock wall is more pleasing to the eye and more attractive to wildlife. Snakes, lizards, salamanders, as well as a multitude of fascinating and sometimes noisy insects, will hide or hibernate in the cavities.

A well-built and slightly inclined wall will last a long time. A good ratio for the incline is one to six (one measure in, for every six measures up). If only round, stream-tumbled rocks are

Plate 22
A rock wall using field stone with lots of spaces and cavities for 'shy' wildlife.

available, you will need careful attention to achieve the proper balance and support. A few well-placed dollops of cement will give additional stability. Spaces and cavities behind the wall, some filled with soft earth or sand, will increase the likelihood of winter and dry season use.

Rockeries using larger boulders (to 90 cm / 36 in. diameter) and similar construction methods, along with appropriate plantings, can also benefit wildlife.

PRUNING PLANTS FOR WILDLIFE VALUES

The objective of pruning is to modify the growth of a plant to accentuate its beauty and usefulness or to increase its flower or fruit production. Pruning is necessary to remove the unwanted, dead, or diseased growth, or to keep the plant to a desired size or form.

When thinking of pruning a plant to improve its use by wildlife, these objectives vary. In addition to improving production,

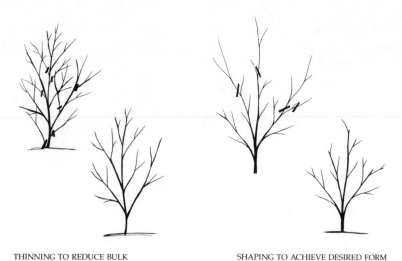

THINNING TO REDUCE BULK   SHAPING TO ACHIEVE DESIRED FORM

Figure 9.1
Two types of pruning - thinning and shaping.

pruning can be planned to provide better shelter or planned nesting locations.

Before pruning, know how that particular plant grows, especially where the flowers and fruits are produced. For example, do these occur on old growth or new growth? For this and other reasons pruning is both a skill and an art.

There are two types of pruning: thinning, which removes entire branches and stems to open up the form of the plant, and cutting back, in which smaller side branches and the tips of branches are removed to reduce the plant's size and produce a more controlled, often bushier form (Figure 9.1). When pruning backyard trees and shrubs use both types of pruning. In addition to opening up a particular plant, consider also encouraging patches of dense foliage. These thick areas are important, particularly as nest sites for some sparrows, finches, robins, and waxwings.

Pruning or removing dead flowers will also extend the flowering period of plants such as Fuschias, Buddleia, and Weigela, which are attractive to hummingbirds, butterflies, and bees.

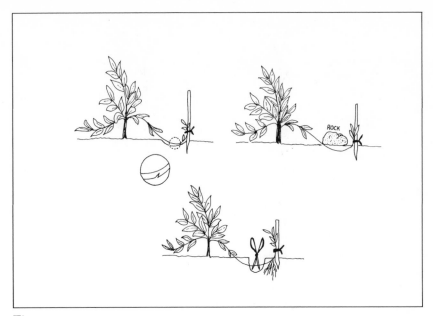

Figure 9.2
Steps in layering a shrub.

ACQUIRING PLANTS FOR THE WILDLIFE GARDEN

Few, if any, nurseries specialize in plants for the wildlife garden. Most, however, have a knowledgeable staff. Using the information presented here and your personal experience, select those species that appear best suited to your needs. Before purchasing any plants, you may wish to talk to the nursery manager. Tell him or her what you are looking for and ask if these plants are suitable for your area and proposed place in your garden, or if there are other species he or she may wish to recommend.

Layering (Figure 9.2) is another technique that can be used to bring desirable plants into your garden. By bending a low branch to the ground, covering it with loose soil and holding it in place with a good sized rock, rooting is often induced. Once rooted, the branch can then be severed and the new plant transplanted to your garden. Red Flowering Currant is easily layered in this manner.

Transplanting is often the best method of bringing native trees and shrubs into your garden. Moving them in early spring

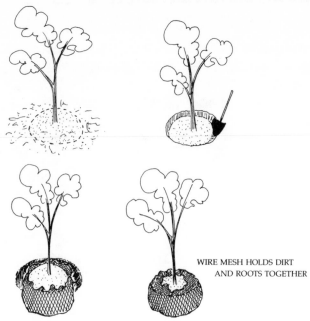

WIRE MESH HOLDS DIRT
AND ROOTS TOGETHER

Figure 9.3
Steps in digging larger plants for transplanting.

or fall produces the best chances for success. Moving larger specimens is often difficult. Figure 9.3 suggests one method that should increase your chances for success.

Cuttings, too, can often be induced to root by dipping the cut ends in a rooting compound and planting them in a pot. Most garden books will describe these and other methods you may wish to try to acquire native and other plants for your garden.

OBSERVING AND KEEPING RECORDS

While scientists such as Charles Darwin and Henri Fabre used their backyards extensively as laboratories, keeping volumes of notes on their experiments and observations, as happy amateurs we need not be so diligent. However, regularly recorded observations become an important diary of your results and achievements.

Such information, when gathered first hand in a systematic manner, has a number of useful purposes. These notes could form the basis for a simple list of the species that visit your garden. They could become a data book of information to assist you in planning future modifications and improvements to your garden. When good documentation is made, the data may help other naturalists or biologists document a species' yearly cycle or life history. Whatever the reason, keeping regular notes will sharpen your awareness and improve your powers of observation.

ABOUT LISTS

While some people might call it a craze, the practice of listing by some naturalists, particularly bird watchers, can be a challenging experience. These lists may be a life-list, a year-list, a provincial-list, or a backyard-list. No matter what the type, these lists provide a simple record of the species seen and identified for a given time or for a given geographic location. While the reasons for listing, using time and area as a base are endless, the adding of a new species or bettering a previous total brings a great deal of inner satisfaction.

Building a Data Bank

Record observations about insects, birds, reptiles, amphibians, and mammals present in your garden. Answers to the questions Who? When? Where? and What? provide valuable insights into what features, plants species, or foods are the most used. Armed with a good number of observations, you can make changes and modifications to your garden that will produce better results.

Notes and Records of Significance

Studies of natural history in the Northwest have been in progress for more than one hundred years, yet it is surprising how little is known about many of the common species.

Because it is not uncommon for amateur naturalists to make significant observations in their own backyards, museums and other institutions are often very interested in having records kept.

Before you contact a museum, have your observation confirmed by a knowledgeable member of your local naturalist club. Due to the great advancements in photography, an acceptable record no longer has to be a stuffed specimen. A good, clear photo with accurate supporting documentation will suffice. If a good photo cannot be obtained, write a detailed description on the spot, without the aid of reference material or books. These notes should indicate time, place, size, and the distinguishing field marks you observe.

What Makes a Good Notebook?

It should have—a hard cover
—lined paper
It should be —large enough not to get lost
—small enough to fit into a pocket
Always keep it handy!

Recording Flowering Times, Flowering Phenology

All flowering plants have an annual cycle which, through simple observation, can be recorded in a systematic manner. This is called flowering phenology. While a number of systems have been devised to record this event, I use an eight-step system that records the stages from the appearance of green flower buds to the presence of ripe fruit or seeds. To simplify the recording method, the following symbols and stages are used.

GB   green bud
FB   full bud
1'F   first open flowers appearing
2'F   secondary flowering stage
       population in first half of flowering stage
       most flowers "fresh"
3'F   tertiary flowering stage
       second half of flowering period
       most flowers "ragged"
4'F   final flowering stage
       last flowers about to disappear
GF   green fruit or seed
RF   ripe fruit or seed

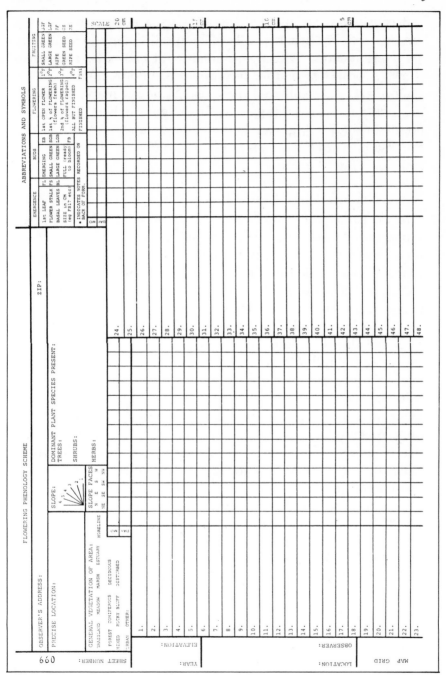

Figure 9.4
A recording form for flowering observations.

Because some of these stages overlap, a double designation can be used. For instance, 2'F - GF indicates many fresh flowers are present along with some green fruit or seeds. Figure 9.4 shows a form designed for recording this information.

Once you have gathered these data, you can map out flowering periods, then endeavor to fill in gaps where nectar-rich flowers would bring you hummingbirds and butterflies. You can also measure from year to year the difference in the seasons and flowering periods.

MAKING YOUR WILDLIFE GARDEN "OFFICIAL"

In the early 1970's the National Wildlife Federation launched a program to establish a nationwide network of mini-wildlife refuges in the backyards of its members. Anyone whose application shows evidence of providing good wildlife habitat may receive a Backyard Wildlife Registration Certificate. Details of this program are available by writing:

> Backyard Wildlife Program
> National Wildlife Federation
> 1412 - 16th Street N.W.
> Washington, D.C. 20036

In the Pacific Northwest, only the Washington State Department of Wildlife has a similar program. To apply for certification, Washington State residents must complete an application that includes a basic inventory of their garden under the broad topics of food, water, and shelter. For information on this program please write:

> Backyard Wildlife Sanctuary Program
> Washington Department of Wildlife
> 16018 Mill Creek Boulevard
> Mill Creek, Washington 90012

Gardens that meet the requirements of this program receive a certificate and a weatherproof sign that can be erected on the property (see Plate 24).

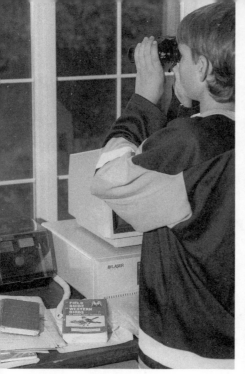

Plate 23
Binoculars, field guide and a notebook—the essentials to observing and recording backyard wildlife events.

Plate 24
Making it "official" in Washington state.

Wildlife for Apartment Dwellers

Just because some people prefer to live in apartments, condo-miniums, or strata title accommodation, they need not be excluded from enjoying an association with some of the common species of urban wildlife. They must just be a little more creative and enterprising. Also, they must realize and accept the limitations which their life style places on the variety of species likely to be present. In the downtown parts of our larger cities House Sparrows, starlings, gulls and crows may be the only link with nature.

Many building owners frown on or even establish rules prohibiting the feeding of birds from windows or balconies. Nonetheless, there are many simple practices that can render an urban apartment much less sterile. After all, if a humming-bird finds your fuchsia attractive, or a House Finch decides to nest in your potted shrub or hanging flower basket, can the occupant be blamed?

Imagine the following case that happened locally in a sixth-floor, downtown apartment.

One afternoon in early spring, the occupant arrived home to find a pair of Canada Geese had taken over a planter on his balcony! Amused at first, he watched the pair construct their nest. Then six eggs appeared, and by this time he had not the heart to evict his new tenants. After all, a Canada Goose gander is not a bird many people would wish to confront, or try to evict from an established nest site.

An impasse arose some weeks later when the eggs hatched. by this time, the balcony nesting geese had become a hot news item for the local press, television, and radio media. Backed up by media personnel, and with the gander temporarily absent, a quick raid netted the female goose and her six goslings. Via the elevator, they were removed to the ground floor and to a nearby pond.

Also, amid the concrete skyscrapers and asphalt roadways of the city, the bright, cheerful song of the House Finch is now commonly heard on quiet spring mornings. Their presence is a reflection of the city's program to "green up" the downtown core. As this greening continues, who knows what other song-birds might appear?

Due to their mobility, birds are the wildlife most easily ap-preciated by apartment dwellers, but the variety of species likely to be observed from windows and balconies will be quite restricted on an annual basis. To many people, these are some of our less desirable species. This category includes House Sparrow, Rock Dove, European Starling, Glaucous-winged Gull, and either the Common or Northwestern Crow. Regard-less of personal bias, these species also deserve our admira-tion. Not only do they survive, even thrive, in a difficult envi-ronment, but also they endure considerable hostile public opinion. For these reasons, their interesting qualities soon can

TABLE 10.1
FOOD PREFERENCES OF 'DOWNTOWN' BIRDS

Species	Foods
Glaucous-winged Gull	kitchen scraps
Rock Dove	wheat, rice, etc.
Crows	kitchen scraps, whole nuts
European Starling	suet, scraps, apples
House Sparrow	chick scratch, bread crumbs
House Finch	peanut butter mixes, or chopped peanuts; sugar-water.

be appreciated. Looked upon in this light, they can bring the watcher many hundreds of hours of enjoyment in situations where few other wildlife distractions may be present.

Many of the ideas put forward in the previous chapters can be adapted or tailored for use near a window or balcony.

Of the three needs—shelter, water, and food—on which all species depend, shelter is the hardest for the apartment dweller to provide. This will depend to a degree on how far above the ground your balcony or window is. A few nearby trees will provide a refuge and jumping off point for many of the smaller species to arrive at your balcony feeder or water source.

Water can be provided either manually or as a by-product from your air conditioner. While a full-sized bird bath may be too large, too messy, or just not feasible, a small attractive water source for sipping or food dunking, in the case of crows, can be considered. If a dripper can be set up, the motion and sound can improve the performance considerably.

TABLE 10.2
IDEAS AND PLANT SPECIES FOR GREENING UP BALCONIES AND WINDOWS

Ideas	Plant Species
Window Boxes	*Fuschia* species Jewelweed
Railing Boxes	*Impatiens* species
Hanging Baskets and Planters	Nasturtium *Tropaeolium* species
Pots and Tubs	Trees Columnar Cedar *Thuja occidentialis fastigiata* Mugho Pine *Pinus mugho mugo* Vines *Clematis* species Morning Glory *Convolvulus* species

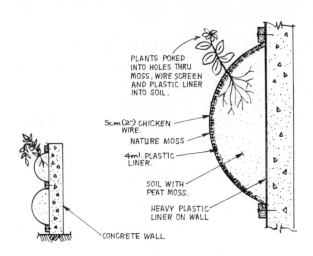

PLANTS POKED
INTO HOLES THRU
MOSS, WIRE SCREEN
AND PLASTIC LINER
INTO SOIL.

5cm.(2") CHICKEN
WIRE.

NATURE MOSS

4ml. PLASTIC
LINER.

SOIL WITH
PEAT MOSS.

HEAVY PLASTIC
LINER ON WALL

CONCRETE WALL

Figure 10.1
Construction details for a tapestry wall.

TAPESTRY WALLS

These vertical gardens, built against a sturdy wall, require strong support and anchors. Behind the fabric lining are pockets of soil (Figure 10.1) in which the plants are rooted. By carefully selecting plants for their color, foliage, and textures you can produce a very attractive wall—to humans as well as to birds and insects. Small green areas among the concrete of built-up areas may become a refuge or rest haven for weary transients during their spring or fall migrations. Like all potted plants, tapestry walls require regular watering and care.

Tapestry walls may also be an appropriate addition to walkways, patios, and building walls or similar blank vertical spaces.

WATER LILIES IN A BARREL

Water lilies and other water plants (see Table 2.5) can be grown successfully in a barrel, or preferably, because of weight, in a half-barrel. These types of planters require a good sunny exposure. Once the "garden" has been planted, goldfish and other pond animals can be added.

FEEDERS FOR BALCONIES AND WINDOWS

By necessity, balcony and window feeders will have to be small. In most cases a flat surface is all that is required. Should you wish to feed small and large birds from the same feeder, the tray for the large birds can act as the roof of the one for the small birds (Figure 10.2).

Hanging feeders such as those available commercially, or a suet bag, are simple and easily maintained.

A NEST BOX FOR SWALLOWS OR HOUSE SPARROWS

If you are lucky enough to have either Violet-green Swallows or Tree Swallows around your apartment, you may be able to encourage their nesting. See Table 4.1 for nest box specifications.

If House Sparrows are in your vicinity, a bluebird-sized box will cater to this species.

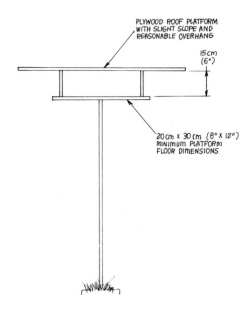

Figure 10.2
A two-story bird feeder.

SUGAR-WATER FOR HOUSE FINCHES

Hummingbird feeders are often visited by House Finches that appear to have a distinct preference for sweetened water. Your local farm and feed store sells a chick fount which can be used to supply pure water for drinking or sugar-water for House Finches. A four-to-one measure of water to white sugar will suffice. (See Figure 4.6 for the details of a sugar-water dispenser.)

Protecting Your Charges and Your Property

In the days when tall television aerials were the rule, it was not uncommon for flickers, our second largest and most abundant woodpecker, to use these lofty perches as drumming stations. Their sound could be heard for great distances, but the quality of the picture on the television set below left much to be desired. In frustration, an acquaintance attempted to solve this annual springtime courtship problem once and for all. Resting his small caliber rifle on the eave of his back-porch, he fired skyward at the offending flicker. His aim was spot on, but not on the flicker. The latter departed hurriedly as the bullet neatly clipped the bracket. This caused the aerial to plummet, puncturing the roof. Did it serve him right? I leave the answer to you.

Protection of backyard wildlife is a two-way street. First, protection for your charges is important because encouraging their presence and supplying them with many of their needs places a responsibility on the provider. Second, because wildlife can cause personal frustration, damage to private property, or act as the carrier of disease, we should be cognizant of potential problems.

Generally speaking, the advantages and recreational enjoyment provided by backyard wildlife far exceed the problems.

PROTECTING YOUR CHARGES

Without any hesitation, Public Enemy No. 1 to backyard wildlife is the friendly, docile, and ubiquitous neighborhood cat. While people who love wildlife have ample reason to strongly dislike this family pet, one must at the same time admire its character and biological efficiency. Everything that moves, from grasshoppers, to reptiles, to birds and small mammals, falls prey to a cat's predatory instincts. No matter how well we feed it, or how often we warn it, a cat seldom can resist the instinct to hunt and pounce on anything small that moves. Cats are ruthlessly efficient predators.

Understanding the magnitude of the problems cats pose to urban wildlife is not easy. One recent study indicated that the house cat was the primary destroyer of chickadees in North America. A second study reported the average house cat kills at least one small mammal or bird per month. Considering the number of cats we keep, simple arithmetic tells us domestic cats destroy hundreds of millions of wild birds and animals annually. The evidence is mounting and wildlife managers are becoming very concerned.

DEALING WITH CATS EFFECTIVELY

With the exception of simple tolerance, there are at least two clear choices you can make to protect your visitors from cats. The first is the erection of a cat-proof fence. The second is the discouragement or the total elimination of the cats.

A Cat-proof Fence

A chain-link fence at least 1.8 m (6 ft.) in height that is snug to the ground. While it may also eliminate raccoons and other larger terrestrial species, it has other advantages. Such a fence provides a good support for climbing vegetation and it sharply delineates property lines. Placing a strand of barbed wire at the top and bottom should only be considered in extreme situations. Barbed wire is dangerous, known to wound or even kill a number of wildlife species.

Cat Elimination: the 1 - 2 - 3 Method

If cats are a serious problem and you feel this problem deserves attention you may wish to try the following plan:

1. *Notify your neighbors* that you are developing and improving your garden as a wildlife sanctuary. Inform them that cats, not necessarily theirs, are causing you concern and that should the problems continue, you intend to do something about it.

2. *Purchase, borrow, or build a suitable live trap* and bait it accordingly. If you catch a cat, and you know the owners, return their pet and mention that should you trap the animal again you will turn it over to the local S.P.C.A. or animal shelter. If you do not recognize the animal, you should ask if someone else does. Should no one know it, take it to the S.P.C.A.

3. *Take the animal to the S.P.C.A.* This method might seem drastic but you would be surprised just how many feral and neglected house cats wander our neighborhoods. Not all cat owners accept their responsibilities. Sometimes they need to be reminded in a straightforward manner.

Traps

A simple box trap is illustrated in Figure 11.1. Suitable commercial traps are available through your local hardware or agricultural supply store. Havahart™ traps have been used successfully with good results for many years.

Traps can sometimes be borrowed from your local S.P.C.A., animal shelter, or from some government agencies.

Protecting Bird Feeders From Cats

The abilities and ingenuity of cats should never be underestimated. To minimize the chances of cats taking birds using feeders, the feeder must be placed at least 2 m (6.6 ft.) above the ground.

While it is more difficult to protect ground feeding species from cats, a number of measures can be put in place. Chicken wire or lathing with 5-7.5 cm (2-3 in.) holes can be placed through vegetated areas or around feeding stations to prevent access and ambush. A similar, free-standing portable screen can be placed across potential direct cat access routes. While

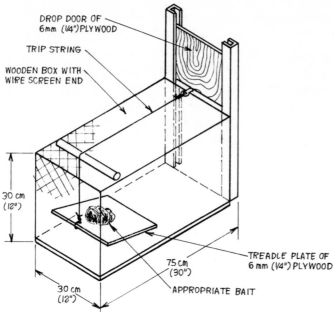

DROP DOOR OF
6mm (1/4") PLYWOOD

TRIP STRING

WOODEN BOX WITH
WIRE SCREEN END

30 cm
(12")

75 cm
(30")

TREADLE PLATE OF
6 mm (1/4") PLYWOOD

30 cm
(12")

APPROPRIATE BAIT

Figure 11.1
Rough plans for a simple box trap for capturing nuisance animals.

these measures may not provide complete protection, they should help minimize the problem.

HAWKS AND OWLS

Cooper's and Sharp-shinned Hawks, shrikes, and in the interior, Northern Pygmy Owls may become frequent visitors to feeding stations. In fact, any area which is developed and becomes a mecca to wildlife will also become a magnet and a preferred hunting location for predators.

Attitudes towards these predators vary to the extreme, but it must be remembered that all hawks and owls are protected by law and cannot be shot or trapped except under permit. Predation is also one of the natural checks and balances that play an important role in maintaining animal numbers. Avoiding predators is part of an individual's day-to-day survival, similar in a number of ways to our daily running the traffic gauntlet.

To protect our backyard visitors from hawks in particular, there are a number of things we can do.

1. *Providing good escape routes:* Feeders and water sources should be constructed and placed to provide a clear view to all possible attack routes. At the same time a 'back door' escape exit or passage should be available. This back door need only be a tangle of branches with passages small enough to prevent a chase. Escape routes should be backed up with enough cover for the intended prey to hide. Around feeders songbirds seem to particularly enjoy a tepee style pile of branches (see Plate 20).

2. *Screens and Nets:* As mentioned under protection from cats, screens and netting with large mesh sizes (at least 5 cm x 5 cm) will permit small birds to enter but will deter would-be predators.

3. *Harassment:* Any time a potential predator, be it cat, dog, hawk or other unwanted pest appears, a sharp rap on a window, volley from a slingshot, or any other distraction, will keep these would-be hunters alert and at arms length. Under this game plan, accuracy is not as important as registering your annoyance!

A BACKYARD SAFETY CHECK

Architects, planners, and home designers are often totally unaware that the creations they design may have serious implications for wildlife. From wells to windows just about everything built into a house or its grounds can have a positive or negative impact on small animals.

Pits, pools, curbs, and window wells with perpendicular sides are traps that many small creatures may enter, from which escape is impossible. If these cannot be avoided, then some form of ladder or sloping ramp should be placed to assist exit. Pools and fish ponds should have a similar shallow egress as part of their design.

ABOUT WINDOWS

More small birds, and many larger ones, are injured or lose their lives by flying into windows than most of us would care to acknowledge. In many cases these collisions only stun the vic-

Plate 25
A window netted with fishing net and the silhouette of a Cooper's Hawk to prevent bird casualties, Bamfield Marine Station.

tim. When these victims are placed in a warm, dry, quiet location the birds often recover quickly and can then be released.

Windows often appear as tunnels, tricking birds either due to reflections or because a second window can be seen through the first. Many solutions to the problem have been proposed with varying results. Some of these are:

1. Pull the curtains to eliminate the tunnel appearance of a second window.
2. Hang strips of silver paper or colored ribbons in front of the window.
3. Place decals on the window to indicate an apparent barrier.
4. Place or hang a netting across the face of the window.

At the Bamfield Marine Station in British Columbia, 10 cm (4 in.) fish net was hung from the eaves and silhouettes of Cooper's Hawks were cut out and hung in the netting (see Plate 25). All of these methods may help reduce casualties.

Where collisions between windows and birds are fairly frequent, perhaps other factors such as the location of feeding stations or bird baths may be a contributing factor. To eliminate the direct flight path, perhaps the feeding or bathing area should be relocated, or a tall tree or shrub placed in line between the window and the area of use.

What To Do With Window Casualties

Birds and small mammals found dead in our gardens often have scientific or educational value. Place them in a clear plastic bag labelled with the date, location, and name of the person who found the casualty. Contact your local museum, high school, or university biology department. Often they will appreciate and have a use for specimens in their programs.

Window-bashing Birds

Each spring, as our neighborhood birds begin their warm-up rituals to their nesting season, some individuals have a terrible time distinguishing between their reflection in windows and a true rival. Watching and listening to this constant bashing is very distracting and distressing. Robins can be extremely persistent in this activity. It is not unusual for them to pursue their supposed rival for several weeks at a number of windows!

Aside from eliminating the bird apparently bent on self-destruction, here are two solutions. Eliminate the perch or perches from which the bird can see its reflection, or hang a large sheet of brown paper outside the window to eliminate the reflection. Even with these measures in place, there is some indication that once conditioned, your bird may search out other windows.

PROTECTING YOUR GARDEN

Should you be a keen gardener eager to produce fruit or vegetables, encouraging birds to come into your garden could prove disastrous. Certainly you do not want to give these potential thieves an open invitation to raid your crops!

Perhaps the most effective way to keep unwanted avian guests from stealing your rewards is to effectively cover your fruit-producing plants with bird netting. Check with your garden supply center about this material. Using netting is not without some risk to wildlife; birds can become entangled and die.

Some bird species, particularly House Finches, start their raiding when your fruit-producing trees and shrubs are in their earliest flowering stages. To reduce or eliminate this early damage, you may have to put your nets up early.

RATS AND MICE

Just as hawks and owls will visit your feeding station with the hopes of finding an easy meal, rats and House Mice will also find your station an easy target. Though these animals are seldom seen, your efforts to provide cover and a high energy food source play right into their hands. When rats and mice become a problem, be careful not to accidentally harm native species. Therefore, please make sure that you can identify rats and House Mice from Deer Mice and voles!

Today, most unwanted creatures are controlled through the use of poison baits. These are indiscriminate killers. When problems arise, rather than using poisons, consider using live traps. These portable units permit the discriminating removal of the unwanted and release of the desirable species. Live traps of appropriate sizes are sold through your local farm supply company. For the unwanted, drowning after capture is a quick, easy, humane way of permanent removal. Poisons should only be used as a very last resort. If you must use them, contact your local Agriculture Office for the latest information on the recommended poison, the suggested dosage, and precautions to be followed.

You may find that with small yards that are neatly groomed and where small native ground mammals, salamanders, and snakes are not likely to be present, the provision of brush piles and cavities will only encourage rats and mice. In these circumstances, these features possibly should not be provided or should be removed.

PROTECTING YOUR PROPERTY

Any vacant space with an external access can become a cozy retreat for a variety of wildlife from raccoons to mud-daubing wasps. House Sparrows, Violet-green Swallows, starlings, bats, and squirrels will all take advantage of small cracks and openings in manmade structures for nesting or roosting.

While all of these species may bring considerable enjoyment, they can also hasten deterioration of your building. They may also bring disease. A careful inspection and repair of the exterior of your building to make it wildlife-proof can provide financial savings and eliminate worries.

BIRDS NESTING IN UNWANTED LOCATIONS

Barn Swallows and robins are notorious for nesting on our buildings. The nests become a messy problem when they are located over doorways or windows.

To stop nesting at these locations before it really begins, place balls of crumpled newspapers in the would-be nesting space. This should force the birds to another, more appropriate location. You may wish to assist this process by putting up an appropriate nesting platform at another nearby location (see Figure 4.4).

DAMAGE FROM WOODPECKERS

Woodpeckers find some buildings ideal sites from which to announce their amorous intentions. Others find hollow walls to be ideal nesting locations. One successful remedy is to place a bag of suet at the site. This food offering displaces the woodpecker's original intention.

Discouraging Nuisance Species

Invariably, when we develop our gardens and put our plans into effect, there are a few persistent and domineering species or individuals which will cause us endless frustration. A number of culprits quickly come to mind. These include squirrels, starlings, crows, jays, gulls, House Sparrows, and wasps. Outwitting pests is not easy, but it can be done.

Three general recommendations for minimizing the problems created by pests are:

1. Provide food these species do not prefer.
2. Provide them with their preferred foods at a second, isolated location where they are less likely to become a nuisance.

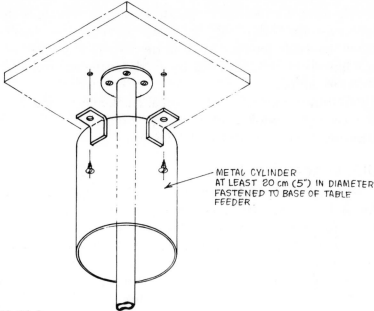

METAL CYLINDER
AT LEAST 20 cm (5") IN DIAMETER
FASTENED TO BASE OF TABLE
FEEDER.

Figure 11.2
One way of squirrel-proofing a free-standing bird feeder.

3. Attempt to exclude them by means of screens or traps.

SQUIRRELS

When squirrels become a pest at a feeding station, they are difficult to discourage. They are also very clever at finding access to your feeders. Squirrel-proofing your feeder is not easy, but it can be done (Figure 11.2). Plastic squirrel protectors using this same concept are available commercially.

To make this really effective, the feeder must be kept away from overhanging branches and other perches from which the squirrel can jump to the feeder.

Perhaps as a trade-off, you can zone your yard and make one area for squirrels only. Supply peanuts, sunflower seeds, or corn with an easy access. Squirrel-proof, as best you can, the areas where they are unwanted.

I once observed an amusing occurrence when a timid Red Squirrel refused to jump to a swinging feeder stocked with peanut pieces. The squirrel could smell them but was frustrated until a flock of chickadees came along and started carting away the kernels for storage. As these flights became shorter, crevices in the bark of the tree where the feeder was located became the birds' favored repositories. This suited the squirrel just fine. The chickadees did the work for the squirrel who was afraid to jump.

Outwitting squirrels can be a real challenge. So much so that a 300-page book, Outwitting Squirrels—101 Cunning Strategems, is available (see Bibliography).

DISCOURAGING STARLINGS AT FEEDERS

Starlings are highly mobile and virtually omnivorous. Around food sources they tend to be gregarious. They also seem to prefer open areas. Because starlings are somewhat larger than many of our seed-eating winter birds, they can often be screened out or away from many feeders by using 5 cm x 5 cm (2 in. x 2 in.) netting. A second idea is to provide only small seeds, since starlings do not normally eat these. Further, place your feeder in an area semi-enclosed by shrubbery and drooping branches. If all these ideas fail, take the feeder away and stop your feeding program for a week. With luck, the starlings will move on to another area.

At Nest Boxes

Starlings prefer a fairly large, deep nesting cavity with a relatively large entrance hole (5 cm / 2 in. or more). While they can squeeze through smaller openings, cramped openings and chambers are not their style. Therefore, to discourage starlings keep your nest boxes small with entrances less than 4 cm (1.6 in) in diameter.

CROWS, JAYS, AND GULLS

The size of these species and their food preferences make them fairly easy to discriminate against. For crows and gulls, a separate and isolated feeding location is advisable (see Zoning in Chapter 8). Jays can be kept away from feeding areas using chain-link fencing or 5 cm x 5 cm (2 in. x 2 in.) lathing screen. In British Columbia, the Steller's Jay deserves preferential treatment as it is the Provincial Bird.

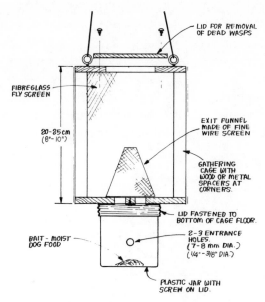

Figure 11.3
Details of simple funnel trap to help control wasps.

HOUSE SPARROWS

As well as being able to tolerate man in large doses, House Sparrows adapt readily to new situations. These attributes, combined with their size and food preferences, make it difficult to outwit them at feeding stations.

As nesting competitors to Violet-green Swallows, they may be particularly bothersome at nest boxes. The modifications shown in Figure 4.3 should alleviate the competition.

ELIMINATING WASPS

Wasps often become a serious pest around hummingbird feeders. However, their quarrelsome nature allows us to keep their numbers in check. By placing a shallow pan of water beneath the feeder, the quarrelling wasps will fall into the pan and quickly drown.

A simple funnel trap (Figure 11.3), baited with a piece of fish or moist dog food, placed nearby will trap hundreds of wasps in a relatively short time (see Plate 26).

Plate 26
Wasp trap with a good catch.

ELIMINATING MOSQUITOES FROM BACKYARD POOLS

Although mosquitoes have a fascinating life cycle, they may not be desirable in garden pools. In large pools mosquito larvae will be kept in check by other animals. If there are areas where this is not happening, the addition of a few goldfish, will make short work of any mosquito larvae.

PROTECTION—A CONCLUDING WORD

The solutions and ideas put forward to solve problems cover only a few major ones that relate to the interaction between man, his habitation, and his desire to have wildlife nearby. Some of the solutions may appear to be drastic, but just as oil and water do not mix, the mixing of many elements we desire or enjoy may be equally unworkable. Finding good and practical solutions to avoid confrontation requires trial and error, patience, discussion, and communication. I would appreciate hearing about some of your creative solutions to these problems.

12

Backyard First Aid—Caring for Sick and Injured Animals

Prepared by Liz Thundstrom on behalf of the Wildlife Rescue
Association of British Columbia

Everyone who takes an interest in animals will be faced, at
one time or another, with the dilemma of having to handle
injured, sick, or orphaned wildlife. At these times it takes a
stout heart and clear head to put reality before emotion. People,
especially those with children, will be presented with these
casualties and asked to solve the problem. In many cases it will
take a miracle for complete recovery. In the presence of young
children it may be particularly hard to adequately explain what
may be the best course of action.

Every year, especially during late spring and early summer,
wildlife casualties increase. This is the time young animals
start to grow up. During this time wildlife rescue agencies,
such as the Society for the Prevention of Cruelty to Animals,
veterinary clinics, and government agencies, are swamped
with calls on how to care for these sick, injured, or apparently
orphaned animals. Despite well meaning intentions and the
best care we are able to provide, the animal dies. Most of these
animals should never have been "saved" in the first place.

However, while the chances may not be great, it may be possible to save the animal if some simple, easy practices are followed. Some of the ways to increase the odds for survival are to

provide a place that is warm, quiet, and dark until help can be obtained.

ARE THEY OR AREN'T THEY ORPHANS?

When a young bird or mammal is found alone, all too often we jump to the conclusion that it must be lost, orphaned, or abandoned. In reality this is usually not the truth. What has happened is that this particular individual has "disobeyed orders" and wandered off, straying into our path. In these circumstances the best thing to do is to leave the truant alone! If you are concerned, the next best thing is to shoo it, rather than carry it, into a nearby patch of cover where it can safely hide. The bond between parents and their young is exceedingly strong. Rest assured that the parents will return and retrieve their offspring.

It is a fact that wild babies always do better with their own mother.

Birds

Baby birds frequently fall or are pushed out of the nest and end up on the ground. The best thing to do for them is to locate the nest and gently put them back. Despite popular belief, birds (and mammals) will not usually reject babies touched by human hands.

If you can't reach the nest, make a substitute from a small box or berry basket lined with tissue and placed as high up the tree as you can reach. This temporary nest should be sheltered by branches from sun and rain. It must also be where the parents can see it, so they can come and feed their offspring. You should watch from a good distance for at least one to two hours to make sure the parents are carrying out their duties.

Once feathered, young birds leave the nest to learn to fly. Depending on the species, this may take hours or days. For instance, crows are very slow and lazy, and it is two to three days before they are flying at all. The youngster will sit on a branch in low shrubbery while the parents call from nearby with a beakfull of food. The fledglings are made to go for increasing periods between feedings. When they are hungry enough, they attempt to flutter and flop to where the parents are. Young birds need this exercise to strengthen their wing and breast muscles for flight.

During this adolescent period, young birds are especially vulnerable to cats. All cats allowed outside should wear a collar with a bell to alert birds to their presence.

Mammals

Mammal mothers such as rabbits, deer, and raccoons often leave their young hidden while they forage for food. Usually the young ones lie quietly for an extended period of time. Rabbit mothers may return only twice a day to feed their babies!

Should you find a nest of baby mammals, or a fawn lying in long grass, observe them from a good distance. Do not approach them closely, disturb them, or try to pick them up. Be as quiet as you can—young animals that are well fed are sleepy. In most situations the baby animals you find are getting fed, even if you do not see the mother around.

True Orphans

There are obvious clues that will tell you if the creature is a true orphan: Is there a dead adult or a number of dead littermates of the same species nearby? Is the animal cold, wet, limp, or thin? Does it look worse than when you last checked it five or six hours ago? Is it in immediate danger? Only if the answer to any of these questions is definitely yes, does the baby need your help to survive.

EMERGENCY CARE FOR ORPHANED OR INJURED ANIMALS

For Baby Birds

Baby birds may be kept in their own nest or a makeshift one of toilet tissue in a berry basket. Place this nest inside an ice-cream bucket with holes cut in the lid for ventilation. Place this on a heating pad or on top of the fridge, out of any draught if possible, since babies get cold easily. They may be fed a mixture of hard-boiled egg yolk mixed with beef baby-food or dog-food. Add water until the mixture is the consistency of soft butter. Young birds will gape for food offered on a toothpick or coffee stir stick and placed as far into the throat as possible. Baby birds in the nest must be fed every fifteen to twenty minutes throughout the day (at least sixteen hours). The nest must be kept clean of droppings. The diet given above is for emergencies only; baby birds require a varied yet balanced diet to grow and develop normally. Natural food items are good diet supplements.

For Baby Mammals

If the animal's eyes are not open it will require warmth and darkness. A nest made of a wool sweater or toque, placed in a cardboard box next to a source of warmth, is best. Babies should be covered but able to move a little within the nest and away from the heating pad.

The rehydrating solution given for birds (see First Aid section below) or Pedialyte™ from the drug store, may be given to the babies for a period of not more than twenty-four hours. Use a pet nurser or plastic eye dropper. Baby mammals need special diets. Cow's milk in any form is a poor substitute, as is human infant formula. If you cannot get them to a care center within twenty-four hours, contact one of the resource agencies in Appendix 1 for further instructions. Do not attempt to give fluids to any animal if it is unconscious.

If the animal's eyes are open, and after giving the rehydrating solution, offer babies small amounts of the appropriate kinds of solid food. You can also give them soya or rice infant pablum mixed with warm water.

Baby opossums, if still in the mother's pouch, are unable to suckle. They need specialized help immediately if they are to survive.

Baby rabbits must be left alone as much as possible and fed only every seven to eight hours. If their eyes are open, do not give them milk; they can eat on their own.

For Injured Adults

Injuries of all types, especially those caused by cats, require immediate attention. As with human injuries, the number one problem is not the injury itself nor the possibility of infection, but shock.

The first thing to do is capture and then quiet the animal. This is most easily accomplished by dropping a towel or jacket over it. Once the head and eyes are covered, it will become quiet and may be picked up. Heavy gloves should always be worn when handling large birds and mammals. Wild animals, injured and feeling cornered, bite and scratch viciously. Consider your own safety. The animal, once captured, should be placed in a cardboard carton as soon as possible and the box put in a warm place or on a heating pad. The top of the fridge or clothes dryer is a good spot for small patients. The box must be closed or covered with a towel or blanket held in place with clothespegs. If it has a fitted top, ensure there is enough air, especially in hot weather. The animal must be kept quiet and away from children and domestic pets. If a bird or animal seems tame, this is a symptom of shock.

Once a patient is quiet, warm, and in a safe, dark spot, find out where you can get experienced help. There will usually be a center or individual in your area who specializes in wild animals. This is extremely important because the care and treatment of wildlings differs greatly from that of domestic or companion animals. The sooner the animal gets appropriate treatment, the more likelihood there is of its making a full recovery and being released back into the wild.

Sources of help include the S.P.C.A., veterinarians, wildlife rescue associations, or, for game animals and birds, your local wildlife authorities.

FIRST AID

If immediate help is unavailable, the following temporary measures may be helpful.

Place the individual in a warm, dark, quiet box for fifteen to twenty minutes. This should enable the patient to calm down. Then offer a rehydrating solution made up of 1 cup (250 ml) warm water, 1 teaspoon salt, 3 teaspoons sugar. Drip this slowly onto the tip of the bird's beak or into the mammal's mouth with an eye dropper, plastic syringe, or plastic straw. Notice whether it swallows. The solution is sticky, so try to keep it off feathers and fur. DO NOT offer it to animals that are unconscious as they may choke or inhale liquids.

This solution will give the bird or mammal some energy and replace moisture loss, especially in hot weather. Repeat every twenty minutes for one to two hours. If the patient seems alert, offer appropriate food and some of the rehydrating mixture in small low jar lids. Notice whether it eats and what the droppings look like. Do not handle your charge—get help for it as soon as possible.

For Birds

Birds that have hit a window should be given the warm, dark, quiet treatment. After approximately two hours, the bird should be checked. If it is fluttering and moving normally, let it out on a screened porch or in a room with windows covered (a bathroom is good) to see if it can fly. If it can manage to lift itself off the ground to a height of at least 1 m (3 - 4 ft.), it may be released from a porch or quiet, safe area. If after 4 P.M., feed the bird and keep it overnight for release early the next morning. If a bird cannot fly, or seems injured, contact an agency or wildlife professional for further help.

For Mammals

If extensive bleeding or a compound fracture is present (bones through the skin) and you are not near a wildlife center, take the animal to a local veterinarian for emergency treatment. If poisoning is suspected, try to ascertain the type of poison and go to a veterinarian quickly for treatment.

Handle adult, injured mammals with heavy gloves and extreme caution. Cartons or pet-kennel cabs can be used as temporary housing. Deer are extremely nervous and difficult to handle. They may have to be tranquilized by a competent person. They may be safely transported wrapped securely in a large sack, blanket, or tarp tied loosely around the neck.

For Reptiles

Injured turtles or snakes may be given basic care for shock. Snakes having wounds from animal attacks can be cleaned and treated with Polysporin™ ointment. Keep them in an old aquarium with a tight lid made of fly-screen. Snakes will eat worms or mealworms in captivity. A turtle with a damaged shell should be taken to a veterinarian for treatment. Release reptiles as soon as possible.

For Amphibians

Frogs, toads, and newts also occasionally need help for an injury or broken limb. Keep them on damp moss in a covered aquarium. They require live food. Small wounds may be treated with Polysporin.™ A broken limb will heal on its own if it is not too badly damaged.

DIETS FOR SICK OR INJURED WILDLIFE

Foods like bread, cornflakes, and a "little brandy" are not healthy for most wild animals. First, determine what species of animal you have. Then you can refer to general references that will tell you the foods in this animal's diet. Seed eating birds will take wild-bird or budgie seed. Hard-boiled egg yolk or beef dog food mixed to a crumbly consistency can be fed to robins, thrushes, jays, and crows. These birds may also be offered cut grapes, apple, or seasonal berries. Warblers, chickadees, and wrens need live bugs and flies like aphids, craneflies, and fruit flies. Many pet shops sell mealworms if you cannot find insects in your garden.

Ducks may be given pellets, grain, lettuce, or grass. Fish eaters may like bait fish or goldfish in a pan of water.

These foods, though they approach the natural diet, are not balanced and should be used for short term, emergency care only.

Severe diet deficiencies are known to cause blindness, rickets, stunted growth, or even paralysis in young animals. Each year numerous wild babies die because of improper or inadequate diets. A deformed or unhealthy animal can never be released back into the wild.

DISEASE AND WILDLIFE

If you encourage or care for wildlife on your property, it is important to be aware that a variety of their diseases and parasites can be transmitted to humans and domestic pets. These include round worms, viral and bacterial diseases such as distemper, salmonellosis, psittacosis, and rabies, as well as ticks, lice, and fleas.

Always take care when handling any wild animal you encounter. Use gloves whenever possible and always wash your hands thoroughly immediately afterward. Wild animals and birds should be kept well away from all other pets and caged birds. Children should be discouraged from handling captive animals—their good intentions create additional stress.

If bitten, cleanse the wound thoroughly with antiseptic and report to your nearest health unit or hospital. If rabies is suspected, the officials may wish to quarantine the animal.

SIGNS SHOWN BY DISEASED MAMMALS

Any wild animal acting in an unusual manner should be approached cautiously or handled with extreme caution. Should the animal appear disoriented, unusually tame, or aggressive, these may be symptoms of distemper or rabies. Squirrels, skunks, raccoons, and bats are prone to these diseases. As rabies is transmitted in the saliva of the infected mammal, heavy gloves should be used and destroyed after use. Animals coming into your care exhibiting these signs should immediately be taken to a veterinarian for diagnosis.

TO KEEP OR NOT TO KEEP 'FOUND' WILDLIFE

The temptations are always great for an individual to want to keep orphaned or injured birds and mammals. You may also be tempted to try to raise wild babies on your own because they are so appealing. However, all these animals require constant and demanding care and proper diets if they are to develop normally. They also need social contact with their own species and training for their release to the wild. If you are sincerely concerned for the animal, get professional help to increase its chances of survival.

Virtually all native, and some introduced birds, mammals, reptiles, and amphibians are protected by law. In most states and provinces it is contrary to the regulations to keep or have in your possession those species designated as wildlife. On rare occasions permission can be obtained. Whatever the circumstances, anyone who comes into the possession of a wild animal should quickly determine what regulations are in effect for their area and act accordingly.

THE BOTTOM LINE

These basic guidelines should help in coping with most wildlife emergencies. Specialized sources of help are listed in Appendix 1. If you act promptly, many of the wild orphans or patients will be able, eventually, to return to the wild, carrying on their species and giving pleasure to future generations of nature lovers.

Appendix: Helpful Agencies

IN CANADA

NATIONAL AGENCIES AND DEPARTMENTS

AGRICULTURE CANADA
Information Department
Canada Department of Agriculture
Ottawa, ON
K1A 0C7

CANADIAN NATURE
FEDERATION
453 Sussex Drive
Ottawa, ON
K1N 6Z4

CANADIAN WILDLIFE
FEDERATION
1673 Carling Avenue
Ottawa, ON
K2A 3Z1

CANADIAN WILDLIFE SERVICE
Environment Canada
Ottawa, ON
K1A 0E7

THE NATURE CONSERVANCY OF
CANADA
794-A Broadview Avenue
Toronto, ON
M4K 2P7

*REGIONAL CANADIAN WILDLIFE
SERVICE*

Atlantic Region
Canadian Wildlife Service
P.O. Box 1590
Sackville, NB
E0A 3C0

Ontario Region
Canadian Wildlife Service
1725 Woodward Drive
Ottawa, ON
K1A 0H3

Pacific and Yukon Region
Canadian Wildlife Service
P.O. Box 340
Delta, BC
V4K 3Y3

Quebec Region
Canadian Wildlife Service
1141 Route d'Eglise
P.O. Box 10100
Ste.-Foy, PQ
G1V 4H5

Western and Northern Region
Canadian Wildlife Service
4999 - 98th Avenue
Edmonton, AB
T5B 2X3

PROVINCIAL WILDLIFE AGENCIES

ALBERTA DEPT. OF ENERGY
AND NATURAL RESOURCES
Fish and Wildlife Divison
Main Floor, North Tower
Petroleum Plaza
9945 - 108 Street
Edmonton, AB
T5K 2G6

BRITISH COLUMBIA MINISTRY
OF ENVIRONMENT
Wildlife Branch
Parliament Buildings
Victoria, BC
V8V 1X5

148   APPENDIX

MANITOBA DEPT. OF NATURAL
    RESOURCES
Wildlife Branch
Box 24, 1495 St. James Street
Winnipeg, MB
R3H 0W9

NEW BRUNSWICK DEPT. OF
    NATURAL RESOURCES
Fish & Wildlife Branch
Fredericton, NB
E3B 5H1

NEWFOUNDLAND-LABRADOR
    DEPT. OF CULTURE,
    RECREATION, & YOUTH
Wildlife Division
P.O. Box 4750
St. John's, NF
A1C 5T7

NORTHWEST TERRITORIES DEPT.
    OF RENEWABLE RESOURCES
Conservation Education
Yellowknife, NT
X1A 2L9

NOVA SCOTIA DEPT. OF LANDS
    & FORESTS
P.O. Box 68
Truro, NS
B2N 5B8

ONTARIO MINISTRY OF
    NATURAL RESOURCES
Wildlife Branch
Whitney Block, Queen's Park
Toronto, ON
M7A 1W3

PRINCE EDWARD ISLAND DEPT.
    OF COMMUNITY & CULTURAL
    AFFAIRS
Fish & Wildlife Division
P.O. Box 2000
Charlottetown, PE
C1A 7N8

QUEBEC DEPT. OF RECREATION,
    HUNTING
& FISHING
690, Grande Allée est (1er)
Quebec, PQ

SASKATCHEWAN DEPT. OF
    PARKS & RENEWABLE
    RESOURCES
Wildlife Branch
3211 Albert Street
Regina, SK
S4S 5W6

YUKON DEPT. OF RENEWABLE
    RESOURCES
Box 2703
Whitehorse, YT
Y1A 2C6

NATURALIST SOCIETIES

FEDERATION OF B.C.
    NATURALISTS
1367 West Broadway
Vancouver, BC
V6H 4A7

FEDERATION OF ALBERTA
    NATURALISTS
P.O. Box 1472
Edmonton, AB
T5J 2N5

FÉDÉRATION DES SOCIÉTÉS DE
CONSERVATION DU QUÉBEC
900 Place d'Youville, Bureau 600
Québec, PQ
G1R 3P7

FEDERATION OF ONTARIO
    NATURALISTS
355 Lesmill Road
Don Mills, ON
M3B 2W8

MANITOBA NATURALISTS
    SOCIETY
128 James Avenue, Suite 302
Winnipeg, MB
R3B 0N8

NATURAL HISTORY SOCIETY OF
    PRINCE EDWARD ISLAND
53 Fitzroy Street
Charlottetown, PE
C1A 1R4

NEW BRUNSWICK FEDERATION
OF NATURALISTS
New Brunswick Museum
277 Douglas Avenue
Saint John, NB
E2K 1E5

NEW BRUNSWICK WILDLIFE
FEDERATION
190 Cameron Street, Room 251
Fredericton, NB
E3B 1G5

NEWFOUNDLAND AND
LABRADOR WILDLIFE
FEDERATION
14 Fairhaven Place
St. John's, NF
A1E 4S1

NEWFOUNDLAND NATURAL
HISTORY SOCIETY
P.O. Box 1013
St. John's, NF
A1C 5M3

NORTHWEST TERRITORIES
WILDLIFE FEDERATION
P.O. Box 495
Hay River, NT
X0E 0R0

NOVA SCOTIA WILDLIFE
FEDERATION
345 Mapleview Drive
North Sydney, NS
B2A 3K4

PRINCE EDWARD ISLAND
WILDLIFE FEDERATION
P.O. Box 413
Souris, PE
C0A 2B0

SASKATCHEWAN WILDLIFE
FEDERATION
P.O. Box 788
Moose Jaw, SK
S6H 4P5

SIERRA CLUB OF ONTARIO
229 College St., Suite 303
Toronto, ON
M5T 1R4

SIERRA CLUB OF WESTERN
CANADA
P.O Box 202
Victoria, BC
V8W 2M6

WILDLIFE RESCUE ASSOCIATION
OF BRITISH COLUMBIA
5216 Glencairn Drive
Burnaby, BC
V5B 3C1

IN THE UNITED STATES

Federal
UNITED STATES FISH AND
WILDLIFE SERVICE
Washington, DC 20240

State
Contact your State Dept. of Wildlife
(or equivalent).

International, National, Interstate
Organizations
(A branch office or affiliate group
may be in your community.)

ALLIANCE FOR
ENVIRONMENTAL
EDUCATION, INC.
Box 1040, 3421 M Street NW,
Washington, DC 20007

AMERICA THE BEAUTIFUL FUND
219 Shoreham Bldg, Washington,
DC 20005

AMERICAN FORESTRY
ASSOCIATION
1516 P Street NW, Washington, DC
20005

AMERICAN MUSEUM OF
NATURAL HISTORY
Central Park West at 79th Street,
New York, NY 10024

AMERICAN SOCIETY OF
LANDSCAPE ARCHITECTS
1733 Connecticut Ave NW,
Washington, DC 20009

THE CONSERVATION
  FOUNDATION
1250 24th Street NW, Washington,
  DC 20037

FRIENDS OF THE EARTH
530 Seventh Street SE, Washington,
  DC 20003

THE GARDEN CLUB OF AMERICA
598 Madison Avenue, New York,
  NY 10022

INTERNATIONAL ECOLOGY
  SOCIETY
1471 Barclay Street, St. Paul, MN
  55106

IZAAK WALTON LEAGUE OF
  AMERICA
1701 N. Fort Meyer Drive. Ste. 1100,
  Arlington, VA 22209

NATIONAL AUDUBON SOCIETY
950 Third Avenue, New York, NY
  10022

NATIONAL INSTITUTE FOR
  URBAN WILDLIFE
10921 Trotting Ridge Way,
  Columbia, MD 21044

NATIONAL WILDLIFE
  FEDERATION
1412 16th St NW, Washington, DC
20036

THE NATURE CONSERVANCY
Ste. 800, 1800 N. Kent St., Arlington,
  VA 22209

THE SIERRA CLUB
730 Polk Street, San Francisco, CA
  94109

URBAN WILDLIFE PROJECT
16018 Mill Creek Blvd.
Mill Creek, WA
98012

THE WILDERNESS SOCIETY
1400 I St., NW, 10th Floor,
  Washington, DC 2005

WILDLIFE INFORMATION
  CENTER, INC.
629 Green St., Allentown, PA 18102

THE WILDLIFE SOCIETY
5410 Grosvenor Lane, Bethesda, MD
  20814

Citizens' Groups:

Bird Feeding Information and
  Supplies
AUDUBON WORKSHOP
1501 Paddock Drive
North Brook, IL 60062

Bat Information
c/o Milwaukee Public Museum
Milwaukee, WI 53233

Selected References

A Note on Common and Scientific Names: In producing this book, the use of the "proper" common and applicable scientific names has been a problem. For insects, mammals, reptiles, amphibians, and birds the reference indicated * in the bibliography has been used.

For native and horticultural plants the names follow:

Flora of the Pacific Northwest—an Illustrated Manual. 1973. C. L. Hitchcock and A. Cronquist. University of Washington Press, Seattle.

New Western Garden Book. 1979. Editors of Sunset Books. Lane Publishing, Menlo Park, CA.

Chapter 1: Introducing Wildlife Gardening—Needs and Considerations

The Importance of Wildlife to Canadians. 1983. Canadian Wildlife Service, Environment Canada, Ottawa.

The Wonders of Instinct. 1918. J. H. Fabre. T. Fisher Unwin, London.

Darwin and His Flowers. 1977. M. Allan. Faber and Faber, London.

"Invite Wildlife to Your Backyard". 1973. National Wildlife Magazine, April-May, published by the National Wildlife Federation, Washington, DC.

Chapter 2: Gardens for Butterflies and Bugs

Rodale's Color Handbook of Garden Insects. 1979. A. Carr. Rodale Press, Emmaus, PA.

The Butterfly Garden. 1985. M. Tekulsky. The Harvard Common Press, Boston.

The Butterflies of Oxen Pond Botanic Park—Their Conservation and Management. 1976. B. S. Jackson. Department of Biology, Memorial University, St. John's, Newfoundland.

*A Field Guide to Western Butterflies. 1986. J. W. Tilden and A. C. Smith. Houghton Mifflin, Boston.

Watching Washington Butterflies. 1974. R.M. Pyle. Seattle Audubon Society, Seattle.

*A Field Guide to the Insects. 1970. D. J. Borror and R. E. White. Houghton Mifflin, Boston.

Aquatic Plants of the Pacific Northwest. 1963. A. N. Steward, L. J. Dennis, and H. M. Gilkey. Oregon State University Press, Corvallis, OR.

Pondweeds and Bur-reeds, and Their Relatives, of British Columbia. 1985. T. C. Brayshaw. Occasional Paper no. 26, Royal British Columbia Museum, Victoria, BC.

Garden Pools, Fountains, and Waterfalls. 1974. Ed. by J. Gillespie. Sunset Books, Menlo Park, CA.

"Semi-domestication of Bumblebees in Saskatchewan". 1980. P. Curry and J. Dalgleish. Blue Jay, Vol. 38, no. 2, pp. 80-86. Saskatchewan Natural History Society.

Chapter 3: Gardens for Small Mammals, Reptiles, and Amphibians

*A Field Guide to the Mammals. 1976. W. H. Burt and R. P. Grossenheider. Houghton Mifflin, Boston.

*A Field Guide to the Western Reptiles and Amphibians. 1966. R. C. Stebbins. Houghton Mifflin, Boston.

The Amphibians of British Columbia. 1984. D. M. Green and R. W. Campbell. Museum Handbook no. 45, Royal British Columbia Museum, Victoria, BC.

The Reptiles of British Columbia. 1984. P. T. Gregory and R. W. Campbell. Museum Handbook no. 44, Royal British Columbia Museum, Victoria, British Columbia.

The Mammals of British Columbia. 1965. I. McTaggart Cowan and C. J. Guiguet. Museum Handbook no. 11, Royal British Columbia Museum, Victoria, BC.

Raccoons. 1975. Canadian Wildlife Service, Hinterland Who's Who series, CW69-4/47. Information Canada, Ottawa.

Chipmunk. 1973. Canadian Wildlife Service, Hinterland Who's Who series, CW60-4/13. Information Canada, Ottawa.

Bat. 1973. Canadian Wildlife Service, Hinterland Who's Who series, CW69-4-12. Information Canada, Ottawa.

General References: Chapters 4, 5, 6, and 7

Attracting and Feeding Birds in British Columbia. 1979. R. W. Campbell and H. Hosford. Museum Methods Manual no. 7. Royal British Columbia Museum, Victoria, BC.

The Hungry Bird Book. 1965. R. Arbib and T. Soper. Ballantine Books, New York.

Attracting Birds to Your Garden. 1974. Ed. by S. Gellner. Lane Books, Menlo Park, CA.

Birds in the Garden and How to Attract Them. 1939. M. McKenny. Grosset and Dunlap, New York.

The Audubon Society Guide to Attracting Birds. 1985. S. W. L. Kress. Charles Scribner's Sons, New York.

Beyond the Bird Feeder. 1983. J. V. Dennis. Alfred Knopf, New York.

*A Field Guide to Western Birds. 1961. R. T. Peterson. Houghton Mifflin, Boston.

Birds of North America. 1966. C. S. Robbins, B. Bruun and H. S. Zim. Golden Press, New York.

Chapter 4: Spring Gardens for Birds

"Hummingbird Flowers". 1973. V. Whitelaw. Discovery, Vol. 2, no. 3, pp. 83-85. Vancouver Natural History Society.

"Hummingbird Flowers in British Columbia". 1975. J. Pojar. Syesis, Vol. 8, pp. 25-28, Royal British Columbia Museum, Victoria, BC.

"Birds and Insects at Sapsucker Workings." 1961. D. Stirling. The Murrelet, Vol. 42, no. 3, pp. 43. Pacific Northwest Bird and Mammal Society.

Nest Boxes for Birds. 1965. W. H. Carrick. Canadian Wildlife Services, Information Canada, Ottawa.

102 Birdhouses, Birdfeeders You Can Make. 1967. H. Sibley. Goodheart-Willcox, Homewood, IL.

Backyard for Wildlife—Spring and Summer Season. 1987. M. D. Dearman. Kerry Wood Nature Centre, Red Deer, AB.

Chapter 5: Summer Gardens for Birds

"Blow Flies and Baby Birds." 1988. R. Cannings. Discovery, Vol. 17, no. 2. Vancouver Natural History Society.

Chapter 6: Autumn Gardens For Birds

The Complete Guide to Bird Feeding. 1975. J. V. Dennis. Alfred A. Knopf, New York.

Chapter 7: Winter Gardens For Birds

"Ten Surefire Ways to Attract More Birds This Winter". 1978-79. G. H. Harrison. Birding News Sur-

vey, Winter Issue, 2-4.
Feeding Wild Birds in Winter. 1981. C. Dobson. Firefly Books.
Relative Attractiveness of Different Foods at Wild Bird Feeders. 1980. A. D. Geis. United States Department of the Interior Fish and Wildlife Services, Special Wildlife Report no. 233, Washington, D.C.
Wild Berries of the Pacific Northwest. 1974. J. E. Underhill. Hancock House,Vancouver.

Chapter 8: Planning Your Wildlife Garden
Invite Wildlife to Your Backyard. 1973. National Wildlife Magazine, April-May. National Wildlife Federation, Washington, D.C.
Birds of Man's World. 1978. D. Goodwin. Cornell University Press, Ithaca, New York.
Planning Your Garden. 1987. A. de Vertevik and V. Burton. Whitecap Books, Vancouver / Toronto.
"Landscapes for Songbirds". 1987. J. B. Burley. *Landsape Architecture,* Vol. 77, no. 3, May/June.
"Landscaping to Attract Birds". 1980. S. Sullivan. *Wildlife Review,* Vol. IX, no. 4, Summer, British Columbia Ministry of Environment, Victoria, BC.

Chapter 9: Gardening For Wildlife
Common Weeds of Canada. 1976. G. A. Mulligan. McClelland and Stewart, Toronto.
New Western Garden Book. 1979. Editors of Sunset Magazine. Lane Publishing, Menlo Park, CA.
Gardening with Native Plants of the Pacific Northwest. 1982. A. Kruckeburg. University of Washington Press, Seattle.
A Gardener's Guide to Pest Prevention and Control in the Home and Garden. 1986. British Columbia Ministry of Agriculture. Victoria, BC.

The Wildflower Meadow Book - A Gardener's Guide. 1986. L. C. Martin. East Woods Press, Charlotte, NC.
"Naturalists and Parks". 1964. R. Y. Edwards. *The Ontario Naturalist,* Vol. 2, no. 2.

Chapter 10: Wildlife For Apartment Dwellers
Ideas for Small-space Gardens. 1978. Ed. by K. L. Arthurs. Sunset Books, Lane Publishing, Menlo Park, CA.
Container Gardening. 1984. Edited by M. Zimmerman. Sunset Books, Lane Publishing, Menlo Park, CA.
"A Photoduplicated File for British Columbia Vertebrate Records". 1971. R. W. Campbell and D. Stirling. *Syesis,* Vol. 4, no. 1-2, British Columbia Provincial Museum, Victoria, BC.
"The British Columbia Nest Record Scheme". 1957. M. T. Myres, I. McTaggart Cowan and M. D. F. Udvardy, *Condor,* Vol. 59, no. 5, Cooper Ornithological Society.

Chapter 11: Protecting Your Charges and Your Property
Trapping with Humane Havahart Traps. 1973. W. E. Sanderson. Havahart, Ossining, NY.
Control of Rats and Mice. 1976. Canadian Department of Agriculture, Publication 1370, Ottawa.
Outwitting Squirrels, 101 Cunning Stratagems. . . . 1988. W. Adler. Chicago Review Press, Chicago.

Chapter 12: Backyard First Aid— Caring for Sick and Injured Animals
City Critters. 1986. D. M. Bird. Eden Press, Montreal.
Care of the Wild, Feathered and Furred. 1983. M. N. Hickman and M. Guy. Kesend Publishers, New York.

The Complete Care of Orphaned or Abandoned Baby Animals. 1979. C. E. Spalding and V. Spalding. Rodale Press, Emmaus, PA.

Wild Orphan Babies. 1978. N. V. Weber. Holt, New York.

A Reference Book of Urban Ecology. 1981. A. I. Dagg. Otter Press, Waterloo, ON.

Index

Admiral: Lorquin's, 13; Red, 13; White, 13
Air conditioner, 75
Alder, 13; creating a nesting snag, 58
Alyssum, 65
Amphibians, 47
Antennae, distinction, butterflies, skippers, moths, 16
Ants, 10, 28; Carpenter, 33
Aphids, 11
Apples, 13, 60, 61, 89, 103; alcoholic, 90
Arbutus, 90
Arrowhead, 19
Ash: Green, 106; Mountain, 89, 90
Aster, 11
Avenues of view, 97

Backyard: first aid, 138; safety check, 128
Backyard Wildlife Program, 116
Backyard Wildlife Sanctuary Program, 116
Badger, 38
Bait, butterfly & moth, 14
Balconies, greening-up, 120
Barren areas, solutions for, 105
Bats, 34, 132; diseases, 46; houses, 43, 45; light to attract, 40; Myotis, 44; rabies, 45
Bathtub pond, 16
Bean, Scarlet Runner, 65
Bee, Bumble, 10, 12, 28
Bee Balm, 65
Beetle: Ladybird, 10, 12; Long Horned, 11
Birch: creating a nesting snag, 58; Paper, 68, 90; White, 68
Bird, food preferences, 85
Bird baths, 72; location, 73
Bird feeders, 78; two-story, 122

Birds, nesting in unwanted locations, 132
Biscuit-roots, 13
Blackberry, 60; Evergreen, 83; Himalayan, 71, 83, 107
Blackbird, Red-winged, 51
Bladderwort, 19
Blowfly, 59
Blue Iris, 19
Box Elder, 106
Box trap, rough plans, 127
Bramble patch, 83
Bread, 89
Bristlegrass, 69
British Columbia Nest Record scheme, 59
Broom, Scotch, 61
Brush pile, building, 82
Buckbean, 19
Buckwheat, 93
Buddleia. See Butterfly Bush

Bullfrog, 35, 48
Bumble Bees, 10, 12, 28
Burgess, Thornton, 83
Burrows, artificial underground, 38
Bushtit, Common, 75, 93, 101
Butterfly, 10, 102; bait, 14; Cabbage White, 13; distinction, skippers and moths, 16; food plants, 13; Lorquin's Admiral, 13; Monarch, 11, 13; Mourning Cloak, 13; Painted Lady, 11, 13; Red Admiral, 13; Skipper, 13; Sulphur, 13; Swallowtails, 13; Tiger Swallowtail, 13; White Admiral, 13
Butterfly Bush, 12, 65, 104, 110
Butterfly Garden, 13

Cabbage, 13
Cabbage White, 13
Canary Seed, 86
Cascara, 71
Casualties, window, what to do, 130
Catalpa, 65
Cat elimination, 1-2-3 method, 126
Cats, dealing effectively with, 125
Cat-tail, 19
Cedar, 60; Columnar, 120; Western Red, 60
Cherry, 103; Bitter, 13, 71; Black, 106; Choke, 90; Nanking, 106
Chick Scratch, 87, 88, 89
Chickadee, 36, 58, 77, 86, 89, 92, 103; Black-capped, 71, 85; Chestnut-backed, 85, 87, 101
Chickadee Balls, recipe, 93
Chickweed, 69, 102
Chipmunks, 34, 37
Cinquefoil, marsh, 19
Clematis, 104, 105, 120; White, 107
Clover, 13; Red, 12
Cod fat, 88
Columbine, 14, 65
Composting, 108
Corn, 103; Cracked, 86
Cosmos, 69
Cotoneaster, 12, 89, 90
Cottonwood, 13
Cow Parsnip, 11, 13
Crabapple, 89, 90, 106; Pacific, 90, 107
Crabgrass, 69
Cranesbill, 69
Crawford bird food, recipe, 94
Creeper: Trumpet, 65; Virginia, 104, 105
Crickets, 10, 25
Crow, 118, 119; Common, 51, 119; food dunking, 75; Northwestern, 119
Currant, Red-flowering, 64, 65

ABOUT THE AUTHOR

Bill Merilees is a native of British Columbia. He holds a degree in Zoology and Botany from the University of British Columbia, and an M.Sc. in Outdoor Recreation/Education from Colorado State University. He is employed as a Visitor Services Officer for the provincial ministry of Parks, and is currently the President of Vancouver's Natural History Society. Bill has published a number of articles on natural history and has participated in several local television series on the subject. In 1980, he received the Elton Anderson Award for outstanding service to the Federation of British Columbia Naturalists.

Bill lives on Vancouver Island with his wife and four children.